SECRETS OF THE ESCAPE ROOM

William Peirson

Dedicated to Steve Krieger

The only engineer who can make fire cold,
slow down explosions, and train moths to act on cue.

CONTENTS

WHY SHARE THE SECRETS OF ESCAPE ROOMS?

Back when I was getting started in puzzle design I went to a lot of Escape Rooms. I remember a trip to a rapidly expanding company that had just opened a fancy new location. We went inside and the lobby looked great with lots of dark woods and their "rewards" program bolted on the wall in custom engraved steel. However, I should have known there was going to be trouble because when we walked in, the last group looked like they had just been told that they had lost their jobs. Watching their sad, crestfallen faces walk past us as I listened to the Game Master explain a confusing penalty-filled hint system should have concerned me more, but I was confident that I could win the room. After all, I had been studying puzzles every day for over a year at that point, what could go wrong? And then they handed me the journal I'd need for my adventure.

The thing about journals in puzzle games is you'd think they make sense. You can imagine clutching the journal in one hand and guiding your team through an intriguing puzzle interface with your other. But what they really do is let the game designers feel free to design some really, really poor puzzles in the room. Puzzles with confusing language and even more confusing engagements. So I ended up flipping page after page as we struggled and argued are way through the game. Were we supposed to retrieve that coin? You had to use a stick to slowly pull it up through twenty tiny slots, so surely not, right? That's not fun. That's incredibly tedious. And we weren't just supposed to guess at the right combination to open a chest with some numbers we had in the journal, right? There had to be another clue showing us their actual order. What's the fun in just guessing from a series of possible numbers?

As the game continued and the minutes ticked by, we were losing hope at ever opening the temple door. We didn't want to use our hints and incur the penalties of the system. So at last, as I was shuffling some planks into the correct position, the clock ran out. The Game Master came in, gently took the journal from my hands, and led us to the promised land of the third room inside the temple. We got to see puzzle after puzzle that would have been really cool to experience. But our own group legacy? Being the next owners of crestfallen faces as we walked out the door. We had now failed at our jobs, so all we could do is make a group of women nervous as they listened to the tedious hint lecture and watched us walk out the door.

For some reason, a lot of the industry prides itself on not being fun for the vast majority of their customers. Customers know if they aren't doing great on the puzzles in your room, you don't have to give them a frustrating limbo of 10 minutes of dead silence before helping them. Or let them spend a lot of precious time arguing about whether or not they need one of the few precious hints they'll receive to help them solve the game. The old school Escape game customers that pride themselves on not being helped are easy to accommodate in more advanced room operations. I introduced the concept of a "hard mode" to my games that gives customers that want to struggle through and possibly lose a satisfying experience while everyone else can has a more satisfying experience too.

A hard mode in a video game will either have more enemies or more objectives for the heroes to solve. In an escape game, a hard mode simply introduces more puzzles or harder patterns. It can even introduce more story elements as players will often struggle the most with a puzzle game's narrative drive. A hard mode can have more puzzles that better incorporate the story, it can revisit puzzles to introduce more complicated patterns, or it can just have a greater number of puzzles in total. It's also a great way to incorporate a large number of guests in a room because there are more puzzles to keep everyone in the group engaged. What hard mode doesn't do is undercut the fact that your players are heroes in their environment.

Because it turns out people love to solve professionally designed puzzles. And they love to solve them as a new team sport. And as it's a new sport we haven't really figured out all the best combinations or rules yet. But as you'll read in this book, there are a lot of ways for us to get started. There's already a lot of secrets on how to build a better escape room, and I'm going to share them all with you. Because I care about the industry and want to see it grow. Because solving an incredible room is amazing fun for people of all ages. But most importantly because no one should ever walk out of a door disappointed in the experience. Especially when we can so easily give them the opposite.

But what exactly goes into designing an Escape Room? What makes one puzzle more fun than another? Well, I'll show a lot of the industry secrets on how it works. There are specific puzzle types, there is 2nd person gameplay, and there are unique narrative expectations to the IPE experience. That acronym is "Interactive Puzzle Exhibit" and it's the first real secret of this book. Because IPE games go beyond the classic "escape" scenarios, as you'll soon find out. Now, we'll want to get away from the "Escape Room" label, so calling them IPEs is more for the suit-and-tie side of this book, but I do think it more accurately describes all the possible puzzle experiences. While the need to escape a trap is one of the most classic narrative structures when it comes to puzzles it is by far not the only one. After all, you crack into a museum, forbidden temple, or bank vault. So if the tension is diving deeper into an environment for the treasure, you're not really trying to escape are you? And picking great narratives is incredibly important to attracting just the right audience for each of your experiences.

Because interactive puzzles are great for all types of exhibits: from museums to classrooms. This technology is just starting to get really people friendly and the best part about that is it can bring us together again when people feel really disconnected from each other. At last we are able to have experiences were we don't just view art but live it.

IPEs are the current apex of live group entertainment. They are the first team sport that involves intellectual challenges and gives their players a higher level of engagement and amusement than movies or video games. Players step into a universe scripted around their presence, tailored for them to personally conquer all its challenges, and become the true everlasting heroes of the story. They live it, and when you live it, it's always more amazing than just watching it. And, unlike in movies or video games, they have a staff that is there to work with them and make sure it's exactly what they are looking for. It's like playing a video game with a butler supporting you the entire time.

To give players the most amazing experience possible I deployed every element of design I could. And when I needed to figure out elements of puzzle design I invented them. This book gives the briefest overview possible (really, I have games I need to get back to designing) of the unique world of IPE games, but my goal was to help you create the best possible games for your players. I've made the mistakes (and boy have I made mistakes) so that you won't have to. And I'll continue making mistakes because I have a lot more ideas to test that might fall flat. But that's what I'm doing: we're here to make you better than me right from the start.

Along the way I'll tell every story about the industry I know and there's a lot of them at this point. I'll never say anything that spoils a room and I've tried to pair every negative story about a room with a positive story from that room somewhere else in the book. If I mention your show in this book as a negative example, well, keep reading. You'll be complimented somewhere. And if I have nothing positive to say about your show you've probably already gone out of business so... hopefully you're over Escape rooms and not reading this? But if you are reading to find out what went wrong, tell you what, that deserves a reward on its own. Have a Red Bull, on me, at my place. And use these secrets to try again in the future!

Introducing IPEs

So what precisely are "IPE's" (Interactive Puzzle Experiences). Well, they are a completely new experience brand with its own set of rules. Which is great because you want your field of work to be its own brand experience. After all, every brand experience produces certain customer expectations and a custom environment to give the customer an optimal experience. It makes you a destination and not just a pit stop.

To better understand this principle, let's examine the brand of the coffee shop experience, more or less the king of custom brand experiences. Really, think about it. Coffee shops have become such an experience that people have become afraid of going there for fear of looking stupid. They don't want to be immersed into the world of coffee, and coffee is just shifting hot water through beans!

The product of coffee starts with the basic commodity of coffee beans. The commodity is difficult for people to gather themselves as it requires the physical and technical challenges of harvesting and processing crops. The product of a finished package of beans, however, is easy for a customer to use and consume. It is available in every supermarket or easily shipped to the customer's doorstep. The only home equipment necessary is a cheap brewing pot. The service of selling a cup of coffee is part of a larger meal and not the sole reason a person would dine at a restaurant. A round of coffee is always optional among friends and family. But the experience itself has overtaken the ease of the supermarket and dining by developing unique expectations for how to best drink coffee and providing customers complicated coffee preparation choices.

Thus we created the specific environment of a coffee shop. Enjoying coffee is usually done while we're trying to work, especially creative work, so coffee shops encourage a special kind of work environment. Coffee can be an especially fun break when shopping so coffee shops are typically in boutique environments. Coffee shops can house all the preparation techniques that, while not creating much additional value to the final product, do increase the performance of ordering a cup. It is fairly easy to stir cream into a cup of coffee, but it is much harder, and much more fun to watch, steamed milk be inserted into the cup by your "barista" from a huge machine of polished bronze. Customers appreciate the "mysterious" work and sensory experience. So much so that the tip jar has become an integral part of the coffee shop experience.

Using this basic formula we can examine how a puzzle experience is built. The commodity is a puzzle, which typically breaks down into the challenge of a lock and the solution of a key. Puzzles have always existed alongside people, and almost all puzzles fit neatly into ten puzzle types, as will be explained in depth later. But once the puzzle is created, it needs to have decorations to really be fun and become a product people are interested in. People love context for their puzzles; to feel like they are engaging the world when solving it. Solving a puzzle is less engaging when it does not include fantastic details. Setting a maze in space or a jungle gives the player a greater investment in conquering the challenge.

The next level is service, in which the puzzle becomes part of a larger story. These are the puzzles encountered in video games. Rarely are puzzles the main aspect of a Triple A game, as that usually goes to fighting, strategy, and exploration, but huge budget games without any puzzle elements at all seem like less of an experience. Audiences expect to encounter the challenge of a puzzle experience when experiencing most forms of personal entertainment.

Finally, the full puzzle room experience works like a coffee shop to bring even more elaborate techniques and the complete theater of puzzles to life. We take everything that existed about games before and push it to a new and even more incredible height, with the experience brand boosting every other level that came before: general commodity, product, and service.

Playing Games

Games are the earliest forms of entertainment, with dice and cards spanning centuries of competitive play. But puzzles themselves have always been solitary experiences: the Sphinx delivers the riddle and Theseus alone answers it. The puzzle is used to prove the qualities of a hero, and as our entertainment evolved, so did the complexity of the puzzles that our heroes solved. The excitement of Indiana Jones solving colorful puzzles in ancient temples instills in us the desire to step into fantastic puzzle environments ourselves and try our own luck at dodging spikes and boulders.

Games are usually competition based: once the rules are established both sides try to dominate the field: either through luck, skill, or brain power. The other players are not rewarded when you win. Playing games together has mostly been scavenger hunts: working together to find a specific list of objects. Or looking over someone's shoulder to give them help in solitaire, wanted or not. Even then, only one person is really playing solitaire and only one person is really finding the object on the scavenger list.

But "team building" exercises are also some of our most ancient rituals. We form a team to toss a football, to sail a ship, to act out a story. The most exhilarating part of being on a team is that everyone has a specific skill that only they can do. The quarterback needs linemen to block and receivers to run before his skill of throwing the ball can even come into play. And as our entertainment evolved to explore more complicated scenarios, so did our stories about teams. The starship Enterprise captured our imagination because it was a crew working together in the final frontier of space. Part of the excitement was watching people perform their roles to solve novel problems: from the ship's chief engineer to the communications officer.

We love to reenact the hero puzzles and the team problems of our favorite stories. We dream of being placed in these same fantastic environments and exploring them for ourselves. And that is what IPE environments give us: the chance to live both moments. They are the next great environment of play. When we watch a movie we are not in control of the action. When we play a video game, we are looking into a world we cannot inhabit. When we are in a theme park, we must remain safely secured to our vehicles. When we enter an IPE world, though, we conquer it as ourselves: we work with our own friends to discover its secrets, live its story, and become its champions.

These are the joys that always need to be kept in the forefront of the mind when designing a room: it is the chance to change an entire world, to play with shiny objects and intriguing toys, to discover classic childhood games in bold new contexts, and to come together as a group and enjoy a well curated experience with heroic moments for everyone. There is no longer a velvet rope keeping us from touching the coolest objects in a museum or a video game avatar to control. You have perfect freedom in the world and that freedom gives you the ability to prove yourself a hero.

This book will examine many things: types of puzzles, elements of expression, tools to test and perfect your room, but the most essential element when it comes to improving your room is this: step back and think "Does this make my customers heroes?" Whatever comes to your mind will be the next step in the right direction. But watch your step. Mastering the art of the heroic is not easy. So let's start sharing the secrets of the adventure now!

THE SECRET OF WHY WE PLAY

—•⊱⊰•—

1st and 3rd person gameplay

1st person gameplay is gameplay viewed through your own eyes. You judge from your own spatial awareness when to swing a tennis racquet or your own mental strategy for what chess piece to move. You can be entirely silent during these activities and don't have to share what you are doing or why you are doing it.

3rd person gameplay is when you are in control of a character. This is the case in most video games, when you assume the role of an avatar in order to perform incredible actions. In the video game adventure series, "Uncharted," Nathan Drake is physically strong and has a sure aim with his weapon even when holding it with one hand and swinging back and forth from a rope with the other. This is far beyond the physical limits of, well, everyone ever. While the world is immersive, you always have unique powers that can only exist because you are playing a special character. And that character comes with quips and sound effects that you can't control.

Playing as someone without any special skills can quickly become boring. Even in Adventure games that limit the character's movement and available actions, they always have interesting or funny things to say or react in surprising ways, like Guybrush Threepwood in the Monkey Island series and his constant attempts to sell fine leather jackets. You're saying and doing things you wouldn't be able to in real life.

The fact that you are playing a character, though, gives you unique gameplay opportunities. You are able to absorb power up's that overcome the character's limitations. And it becomes easier to reset and try again when you are not forced to undergo the tedious nature of 1st person experiences, such as fetching tennis balls to keep practicing your serve or resetting the pieces on a chess board. You also never need to make time for showering, cleaning, or paying the bill for property damage.

2nd person gameplay

With their being such clearly defined 1st and 3rd person gameplay we have always had the question of if there is "2nd person" gameplay. In novels, after all, it is easy to accommodate three different types of narrative person. While novels started with the "he" of story protagonists, authors eventually began to use the "I" of first person to insert immediacy as well as subjectivity and uncertainty into their stories. This uncertainty was later expanded in "choose your own adventure" stories, in which "you" are able to make decisions, or at least make a limited number of choices to help make the story more "yours." But 2nd person narrative doesn't really exist. There is no way to accommodate "you" besides giving you limited choices. You're still reading yourself as a character. "You" can't exist in the story.

Your personal history and skills are not being used to "choose your own adventure." You can't step into a true hero role that requires extraordinary skills to keep the choices and story interesting. You aren't really inhabiting the space of the video game.

Another issue is the lack immediacy. You need someone else telling "you" what to do for 2nd person gameplay and so that means you are never responding in the immediate moment. You have to wait for the narrator to give you choices. If you are not lifting the rope exactly when you want to then you are still playing someone else's game. You need to depend on and work with another person and their own point of view. True 2nd person gameplay will accommodate making decisions as a group while still accommodating the immediacy of the individual. You need simultaneous communication and action. The fun becomes complying with (or issuing) commands to win.

IPE games deliver all the requirements of a true 2nd person gameplay experience. You play in the room solving puzzles and following the instructions of your teammates. Almost every IPE game requires a team of players, because part of the fun is seeing and responding to how other people think through the challenges of the room and how they help you with your own ideas. You don't just play but you perform as you move objects, step onto the right place, and unlock treasure chests.

Additionally, it is always possible to switch roles so you can better understand what the other person is seeing, thinking, or doing. If you fail in a video game, you reset the game to try again. But in an IPE game, you do not "reset" the world of the video game avatar but "reset" your perspective to see the challenge in a new way.

If you are having too difficult of time in a game, you can get a power up or even a cheat code to push past certain challenges. In IPE games, the power up's that you can enjoy come from the skill sets of other people which can help you "leap" past limitations. You are able to enjoy the speed of people working together to solve a problem and the immediate advancement of having other people help you with tasks. You learn new facts about your teammates and can come to respect them more. You can also learn more about their limitations which can lead to more funny moments to regale yourselves with while enjoying an after-game drink at the bar. The more a room emphasizes the 2nd person gameplay, the more it takes advantage of the unique opportunities of IPE brand experience.

Essence of a Story

There have always been stories that centered around puzzles. Solving murder mysteries, uncovering lost treasures, or finding the secret weakness of an evil empire. Each of these stories inspired us visually as well as emotionally. Goonies. Indiana Jones. Treasure Island. Star Wars. Theme parks thrived by fulfilling our desire to live out these movies by giving us the vehicles we need to dive into their worlds. Vehicles we were locked into and couldn't get out of, sure, but vehicles none the less.

Those fantasy worlds work best when we believe the odds are impossible against our heroes. And nothing builds those odds more than the strange characters and hostile environments that force our heroes to change and adapt in order to meet the challenges placed before them.

A story compresses time and space: we jump from exciting place to place because the essence of all drama is action: the need for it, its execution, and its aftermath. The higher the magnitude of action, the more exciting the story. Shocking deeds, profound discoveries, life altering situations: we love them all because they present the unusual situations we don't see in life. When we first watch them they give us the highest possible entertainment of novelty. What we desire most is a satisfying ending to our story, and everything should build towards that ending. It should all be about the final explosion.

But there is a diminishing return to the great stories cinema has created. As we see variations of the same story again and again we slowly realize that all hero movies kind of blend together. Try to find a Marvel movie where the hero doesn't fight a "shadow" version of himself at the end and you'll be left with less movies in your hand than the infinity stones. So the new great novelty we need is living the story ourselves. We need our battles to have that fundamental drive of action and those unexpected surprises of discovery to return our interest in them as the prime form of entertainment. If we can no longer expect those drives and surprises from the movies of Hollywood, then we need to build them. If we are building to our own special endings, then we will always be satisfied with it, even if the explosion is as simple as some flashing lights. Because there is something about defeating the dragon yourself that is always more engaging than watching someone else defeat it. Truly living these moments with your friends gives them a quality that can't be topped.

Hero's journey

The most successful story is the hero's journey. It introduces conflict, the ability to resolve it, and then how to return to the ordinary world in a perfect circular arc for the hero to follow. The Hero's journey always begins with the ordinary world. The hero has something special about him that sets him apart from his everyday life and makes the everyday unsatisfying. The call to adventure is the introduction of the conflict of the story. This is the explanation of the strange world that the hero must journey to in order to save the day but also prove his worth in ways he cannot in the ordinary world. While the hero has great skills and power, in the ordinary world there is no need to apply them as the world is already established and safe. It is only by stepping into the spectacular that the hero has a chance to really prove himself as extraordinary. This means that the special world must have dangers and challenges unlike anything he has ever seen or could ever prepare for. It's not much of a hero's journey if he must travel to a strange world to help them with their tax forms.

The next step of the hero's journey is meeting the mentor, someone who knows the dangers of the special world and can prepare the hero for them. This is an inhabitant of the world, but without much of an active part in it, usually because he is too old to try and be a hero, but it can also be because it is not his "destiny" to be the hero and he respects that it is the hero's fate to save the world. There may even be training the mentor provides to the hero to prepare him for the strange new world, using everyday materials that serve as a basic introduction to the fantastic adventures the hero will soon face. The mentor leads the hero to the threshold, but the hero crosses the threshold on his own.

When the hero has freely crossed the threshold, he has chosen to battle and going back to the ordinary is no longer an option. He will now prove himself or perish. The crossing of the threshold is the point of no return, and there can even be a physical block preventing the return to the ordinary world, such as his ship being wrecked on the shores of this dangerous new frontier. The hero must now depend on the resources he has brought with him. The time of preparing with the mentor is over and the only role the mentor may now take is watching from the shadows.

The special world the hero enters can have its own rules and customs. Even aspects of daily life that are taken for granted, such as physics and the weather, can be different in this world. Magic and the impossible should thrive there, after all, because it must be different than anything the hero could ever have experienced before. The more disorientated the hero, the richer the story. Some hero stories, such as "Alice in Wonderland" have become great from the strangeness alone, as Alice does not battle or conquer Wonderland and instead simply tries to understand it.

The hero will encounter tests of his character, surprise allies that will help him improve, and inevitable enemies that he must overcome. Everything will lead to his final victory and the reward that proves his status permanently. It is at this point the hero returns back to the real world with his new riches, completing the circle by leaving the fantastic for the ordinary. He has finished living in the spectacular and is ready to return to the steady rhythms of the everyday. Only when the hero can relax and be at peace do we know that the story is truly over. He no longer needs to prove himself or have another adventure but can instead enjoy his reward and, perhaps, be a mentor to the next hero when that time comes.

Player's journey

The same arcs and journeys exist in every IPE. Players encounter every part of the hero's journey, but their tension comes exclusively from solving puzzles. Every puzzle has its own narrative of struggle and success, with exciting discoveries and rewards. The players only need one trait to make them into heroes of their game world: the ability to solve puzzles alone and as a team. The call to adventure for an IPE will be the advertisements of the game requesting the players come and save the world. The more the advertisements present themselves as a true quest of worth, the more players will want to prove themselves as heroes.

In an IPE game, the game host is the mentor character. He leads the players to the world and gives them the context of the story as well as trains them on how to survive it, such as how to contact their ally the Game Master for hints. He presents himself as a natural part of that world that has stepped over the threshold to meet the players. He is the first character the players meet and will be a part of the story for the entire experience: never breaking character so the players believe they are truly living the story and truly crossing over into a new environment.

The players cross the threshold when they enter the world and see its strange wonders, and they cross the point of no return when the countdown begins. Now they have a clear chief opponent: the time limit set on their ability to prove themselves as heroes in the strange land. This is why it is important players get the chance to choose whether they are playing a game on easy or hard. Some people might like the ability to be truly defeated, but many will prefer to be challenged but still be confident that they will complete the story. Playing on easy or hard will affect how much help they receive from the world as well as how daunting the obstacles are that they experience. But, most important, if they do lose their game then the strange world loses its life and, at best, becomes frozen in time. One Escape Room I know would do "just kidding" voice overs to try and complete the story but it still feels like a real let-down. To interrupt the hero's journey is one of the most jarring stops of a story and you have to be certain that your players truly want that risk before providing it to them.

Players will encounter tests the same as the hero, but their enemies will usually be unseen so as to not break the illusion that they are actively involved in the world. The allies they interact with can also be characters from the world, but more often it is the Game Master contacting them to give clues when they are stuck. That doesn't mean the Game Master has to contact them through a game breaking video game screen, however. It is much more fun for players to receive "true to life" help, such as a voice over from characters in the game or through handwritten notes or phone calls. It helps players enjoy the quest to have a constant sense of support and to know that while they are the chief ones struggling they are never completely on their own. This will build into the reward the players get at the finale of the game and their final victory. Even if they fail to reach the climax on their own(in easy mode), the Game Host should step in and lead them through the final challenge so that they still leave as heroes. It is the peak-end rule of commerce: both the most intense part and the end of an experience influence people's opinion on the activity the most. If the ending of the game is a satisfying climax that clearly bestows hero status to the players before returning them to the everyday world, then people will have a fond memory of the game. If what they really want is a challenge that can best them and demand they return another day, then that is the experience that should be provided. But rarely do people want to watch puzzle after missed puzzle in a final breakdown by the game host. Either they should be guided to a final success or they should truly embrace a defeat.

It is at this point the players return to the real world with a souvenir to prove their success, be that a group picture, a winning time on the wall, or just their memories. When the circle is completed successfully, it helps cement the adventure in the minds of the player. That is why the experience could continue with the Game Host escorting them in character back to the real world. That aura of performance keeps the sanctity of the world intact. Keeping the magic of the environment as much as possible keeps the memory of the experience pure. Of course, many players at that point enjoy a peak behind "the curtain" of the experience after the game is over, so it is up to the staff to decide the best experience to provide to the heroes on the completion of their journey: that of behind-the-scenes or that of being a true champion.

Learning from stories

The hero's journey becomes more interesting when the character pairs with the challenges in interesting ways. How can a scoundrel win honestly? When will a hero compromise his principles? People don't like rigid construction: the same challenges tackled by the same perfect characters. But they don't want perfect freedom from heroic structures either. Novelty can make up for the limitations in freedom. Once you know how to drive, it is the changes on the sides of the road that keeps things engaging. You enjoy watching as the town turns to a forest, a desert, or a bustling city. But you want the road itself and the rules of the road to stay the same. We are already trained for certain patterns by video games and movies and we want them to remain the same when we experience them ourselves.

When we see variations in the hero's journey we are learning again after having mastered a basic pattern. Good teachers make learning fun because they know how to give the students a sense of variation instead of the tedium of endless problems that are about the same subject.

The heart of learning through stories is being taught who we are or who we should be. They teach us what choices to make and why to make them. But we quickly master basic morals and so want our stories to show us interesting variations. We know the basics of survival: find shelter, food, and water. But how do we survive in a desert versus a jungle or on a space station versus the bottom of the ocean?

Games go further and teach us how to make the choices that stories display. Games themselves used to be used chiefly to teach how to be moral and to emphasize the moral lessons of stories. Most ancient games have military and religious backgrounds. In general games are always presenting us with the model of real things but highly abstracted. Monopoly is fun because it feels like you are truly traveling through a city and purchasing an entire city's worth of property. Monopoly was supposed to teach the moral that the endless capital grind was not worth pursuing: instead it taught the moral that money's always fun if you have enough of it.

Games, after all, give us the power and control to test out the morals for ourselves. They help us quantify, reduce, and classify. They help us focus exclusively on actions and not the emotions or philosophies behind them. They help us find the objective in our experimentation. Players spend their time ascertaining patterns and ultimate goals.

We are trained to learn, play, and discover in our games so that we uncover the novelty ourselves. IPEs offer a combination of collaborative and solo gameplay that invite participation as well as observation. They bring us back to primal activities that were always the essence of gameplay.

Games will almost always bring us back to the primal idea of expanding our territory and using the lessons we have learned from stories to do so. An IPE game is territorial in so much that you keep expanding the area you have conquered. Expanding territory is the principle found in almost all games, either "to get the other side" or to "explore every inch." Getting to the other side means to keep moving and conquer all the challenges in your way. This informs everything from the earliest 1980s video games of Frogger and Donkey Kong to the triple A titles today of Uncharted and Medal of Honor. Exploring every inch of a game started with Pac-man and continues with the standard of collectibles that exists in games from The Last of Us to Mario Galaxy.

In fact, the idea of territory informs most of our "power ups" in games. Getting extra time to accomplish what you need to. Discovering secrets in the world. Getting tools that help you explore. Getting weapons to conquer the enemies in your way.

This idea of exploration and conquering challenges has kept a lot of activities alive even in the age of video games. Haunted Houses let us explore interesting environments as we face the enemies of people trying to scare us. Museums offer ground to cover as we try to see all the exhibits. And marathons give us a challenging "other side" to reach. But when we explore we want either want to conquer or we want to explore perfectly and so IPEs challenge on a deeper level.

Fun in learning

We learn by watching stories and by the time we are adults we have their basic lessons mastered. Now we can combine learning them again into a novel new experience. Fun is practicing and learning, not exercising mastery. Anticipating a solution can be as exciting as applying one when you are learning how to apply a skill and not just solving something you have already mastered.

There are activities we can do without any help because we have mastered them, activities we cannot do because they are beyond our abilities, and activities we can do with some help. Fun tends to come from the last one. The support we get can be from luck, hints, or even special power-ups.

Games are often trying to teach techniques and particular perspectives. There is the underlying human desire to get better at things.

To know your environment and be the best at it. Fun games require a range of abilities. Checkers seems like it is just jumps but it is also about forcing your players to make a move. Learning the different skills you will need over time and not all at once makes the game more fun.

Highly experienced players should still get the same amount of fun as inexperienced players in a well constructed environment. This means that puzzles should never favor mastery. They shouldn't require a high-level understanding of mathematics, code deciphering, multiple steps, or high lateral thinking. These are all skills that players master after playing multiple rooms but the average person would deeply struggle with when playing them for the first time.

Success, after all, is a literal pleasure. Even if we were the ones who lost our keys we take pleasure when we find them again. And because we have the capacity of imagination we can take pleasure in mental successes as well as physical ones. The brain craves learning, but not to the point of exhaustion. Which is why reading about other people learning can be fun. We can enjoy imagining successes and reading other people identifying patterns. A book that fails to lead you to the next chapter has boring and predictable patterns.

The brain never wants to uncover an entirely new system and it also doesn't want to endure an environment without a system. That is why we try and find the balance between deprivation and overload, excessive order and chaos, silence and noise. Because between silence and noise we find music.

That's why it is fun to find a game of tic-tac-toe in a puzzle environment in a new context but without explaining the principles. The pattern is simple enough that we are able to pick it up instinctually but not so complex that we get lost in the possibilities. Novelty comes from rediscovering the familiar: a game dynamic we mastered as a child.

Stories provide novelty by presenting different emotions and philosophies. Does the gruff detectives worldview actually fit the world? Will the optimistic nanny bring order to the household? They can rarely give us the novel from actions alone and, if they do, they have to give us spectacularly colorful actions to maintain our interest. Games let us live the extremely high stakes of stories but without consequences. We can have fun trying to disarm a nuclear bomb without dealing with the fallout if we fail. Fun is learning, winning, or losing in a context where there is no pressure from consequence. We want to be able to practice in an environment that gives us the illusion of high stakes but the reality of novelty.

The eternal hunt for novelty

Finally, the hunt for novelty can surprise us because we are able to find novelty in the most surprising things. Why is it more fun to multiple some numbers than others? 7x7, 5x5, 2x10 each contain an elegant surprise can teach us a lesson as we search for beauty.

7 x7 is 49. That feels random to the human soul. Why so close to the whole number of 50 but not complete? And how do the sevens even get there as "49" feels so far away from what a set of seven might contain. The randomness of it makes us look back at the number and examine it again. Novelty can come from random elements.

5 x 5 is 25. That feels complete. All the fives you could ever need and stacked against each other. It is a perfectly sized grid in our mind. Novelty can come from neat complete sets.

2 x 10 is 20. That gives us structure and speaks of clear sets. It shows us evenness even in the first "big" double digit number. These patterns help us find the abstract and the iconic. They are simple enough to be absorbed easily but engaging enough to be fascinating to people of any age. Novelty can come from function.

These numbers bring us the beauty of patterns. And patterns themselves are an incredibly important essence of gameplay. A pattern in not just one thing after the next but a different thing that is expected. Life comes in more varieties than the mind can ever comprehend, but the basic pattern of birth, growth, decay, and death immediately grounds are understanding and helps us understand spring, summer, fall, and winter. There are certain levels in a game that are always to be expected because that fit the pattern of alternating the basic controls.

IPEs take the general active verbs of games and add to them the active verbs of pattern making. Now, to pursue the active verbs, we work together as a team that searches, infers, communicates, and resets. There is a difference between learning a completely new experience and parsing new data. When we work as a group in the context of solving puzzles it helps to encounter familiar arcade controls, tools, and simplified games. But we are discovering them in exciting new contexts and by working together. We have created the team sport of gameplay. You get lost in the experience and work in the experience as a group.

Games do not provide innovation and invention, but patterns and progress. People like when things get easier as it goes. And more efficient. And more predictable. So it is best to pattern your puzzles from that perspective.

Unpredictability should be given in predictable ways: with foreshadowing or established narrative structures. The more the unexpected feels natural to the world the more it falls into the pattern we have already created with our minds.

THE KEYS TO THE ELEMENTS OF EXPRESSION

Everyone who plays a game knows it. There's that threshold moment when you step into a new room that sets up so much about the experience. What's the first thing to rush over your senses? Do you see a possible puzzle to rush to when the game host finally leaves you alone? Are you excited to be in a lush environment that promises surprise after surprise, or are you disappointed to be stepping into a warehouse or office park structure with some amazon boxes with tiny locks in the corner?

Try as you might, it is impossible to experience an environment all at once. One moment is not enough to see all the structures and artifacts in a location. While we may have an instant impression of a mountain view or a work of art, they both take additional time and consideration for us to appreciate all of their aspects. We can even overlook important details for years and be startled when someone else points them out to us.

Great artistic expression invites contemplation, like a movie poster that has our eyes darting from detail to detail. Does the story look like it will be funny, exciting, or sad? Does it promise surprises, stunts, or emotional resonance? Or does it hint that it will be a stitched together mess of clichés and not worth your time? One simple poster has many energies to convey: that of expectation and reality, the story of the world, and the story of the production itself.

And a picture is just a thousand words! In places we visit, there are additional dimensions, such as moments of compressed activity waiting to be released. You don't really appreciate a restaurant until you are served the chef's food, and you don't really understand how someone uses their kitchen until you look in their fridge. You don't really know an instrument until you hear it play. The hidden potential tells you the most about the existence of a place or thing. A useful kitchen has prepared stations and equipment for setting up, cooking, and cleaning. The better the kitchen the more each activity has been considered in a linear sequence and the more fully it can be expressed by the cook.

Going even further, the dynamics of the environment can change dramatically during use. A used kitchen shifts from the clanging of pots in the preparation, to the smells of food in the cooking, to the heat of hot soapy water in the clean up. We appreciate the place more deeply as we experience it's continuing shift in dynamics. Even a moment as simple as sitting on a garden bench changes based on the time we set there: in the morning as the birds chirp and the world bustles around us or late at night by a crackling fire and the soft quiet of a world at sleep.

In IPE games people demand way more dynamics than they get in a garden. They should feel that they are stepping into a world has been specifically made for them. Their actions should control every aspect of the world and each of their accomplished goals should cause the world to react and reveal all its hidden potential. The challenge of the physical and mental meld to make a unique interactive experience.

IPE games are a new level of stage design. The principles of expression that people enjoy as an audience remain, but now they are able to step onto the stage itself and play with its elements. A theater's stage is made to draw our eye to the action, so an IPE stage should guide us into the action. Every action expected should be possible so the greater freedom demands more careful design because you cannot place limits on the new play environment, either with unnatural barriers or marked instructions. In video games, the most frustrating barriers are the obvious ones, like a tree that's fallen over a path. Players know they could easily hop over the tree, so it's easy to recognize the designers lazy attempt to block them. Similarly with IPE environments. Environments don't have instructions or limits: they just are. So having an environment with noticeable limitations, such as locked doors that are never a part of the game, becomes frustrating to players.

I've been in rooms that are barely converted office spaces and they've felt like it. If I feel like I should be clocking in for my shift then the room has fundamentally failed to transport port me to an expressive place. Yet, and this is the great thing about IPE games, I don't have to be transported to an expensive place. Just a place that has been thoroughly thought out. Some boxes in the corner and a quickly painted mural on the wall take me half-way to the pirate ship. If the room is clearly full of expression, then the puzzles will complete the rest of the experience. That's why it is important to make sure every element is expressed.

There are a lot of different elements of expression to consider in a room. Each element is like a different body part: some tell us more about who a person is than others, but all of them are important to identify a complete person. The more a room can function like an independent being, the more it will feel naturally vibrant.

More importantly, analyzing every element of expression independently will help you realize if one element is not working harmoniously with the others. If even a single instrument in an orchestra is playing a different melody the entire symphony is ruined. However, an orchestra can be overwhelming if every instrument is considered all at once. Some instruments are obvious, like if the cymbals clash at the wrong moment. But the single out-of-tune viola would be impossible to find if you didn't know how to examine and adjust the isolated component.

Finally, some of the best elements are the ones that change throughout the course of the game. Shifting colors, lights, animation, and sounds all work together to increase the dynamics for your players. All stories are stories about great periods of change, so the more your room actively changes during gameplay the greater the room.

Color

Color gives us our greatest clues to the room's theme. Heighten the chroma of color in a place beyond the normal and typical and people instantly feel they are someplace special that deserves their attention. Colors are also your best friends for portraying transitions in a journey. As your players progress, they can journey from light to dark, from monochromatic to technicolor. Every journey of color is one from the everyday to the fantastic.

In the choice of color, most of the work has been done already for you. It's important to use already established palettes of popular video games and movies. People want to step into the worlds they already love, and nothing portrays a certain reality better than matching the color they saw on the poster or box. It's not Resident Evil's Raccoon city, you just so happen to shop at the same paint store!

Color can also be used to substitute other elements that are difficult to control. For example, the color of waves on the floor replaces the need for actual water. Using shimmering lights to heighten the color experience can give a great sense of movement that standing water would be difficult to control.

The blending of colored lights can also bring greater complexity to a projected outside environment beyond what the players are experiencing. When we glance at a window, we expect the colors of the outside to be rich in complexity because there are different objects that can be seen. Instead of setting up those objects, simply adding multiple light sources by the side of the window can produce enough of this effect to have the imagination take over the rest.

The contrast of colors can also bring greater depth to the shapes in an environment. The melancholy of the blue in round circles on the rocks in a mysterious cave becomes greater when contrasted against the functional brown squares rocks also scattered in the environment. An environment of simply gray rocks doesn't provoke a mood of either warning or utility. A castle of normal colors may be regal, but a castle with the warmth of purple in the walls and shimmer of gold on the ceiling feels like a fairy tale.

Lighting

Lighting is the best way to express movement in an environment without using more expensive equipment. With the ability to shift in intensity and highlight different sections over the course of a game, lighting encourages exploration as the beats shift through the story. A cavern can feel like it is collapsing by simply creating new limitations on the visible light. Lighting can also help conceal and reveal portions of the game and let players know what areas are active or special. A city street in darkness is less likely to be explored by the players than a bright, inviting casino front. Unique lighting, such as patterned lights, can project intriguing shapes and mysterious moods. A warehouse becomes more mysterious with grated lighting projected onto the floor. Lighting is also great for emphasizing rewards, like calling attention to a newly opened treasure chest and Spotlights are always useful for giving players gentle hints about what they should do next.

While color can generally portray the tone of a room, they can never be changed. The lighting however, can add specific mood shifts as quick as a flash of lightning or as slow as the rise of the sun at dawn.

The immediate danger or relief lent by casting more intense hues and shadows will do more to bring the room to life than even the greatest of animatronics. Large, sweeping changes can depict large shifts in nature. Sparse lighting portrays a perilous place full of risk. A flood of neutral lighting can portray a bland workplace, and carefully placed intricate lighting portrays the contours of a luxurious palace. And, best of all, almost all the lighting shifts can be controlled directly by the players actions, giving them a sense of control in their environment that cannot be replicated in any other experience.

In my haunted theater game, when players activate the stage lights before performing the final dance it gives them a great sweeping element that adds distinction to the climax in no other way. All we needed was to have some out of place light stands and LED spotlights to provide an exciting and engaging finale.

Indirect lighting

Indirect lighting is ambient and creates the general mood of the game. The lights will either be hidden in the environment or placed at a distance from active game play areas to avoid the direct line of sight of the players. The easiest example would be lights recessed into the ceiling, but this can also be lights shining through gauze or hidden behind neutral props and barriers. Basically, there should never be an easy way for the players to interact with the light or lighting equipment itself because it diminishes the reality of the game.

Indirect lights can also take advantage of their distance from players to cast more elaborate shadows and convey a greater depth of space. Shadows cast on a floor will make a warehouse environment seem taller and multi-level, even though players will never leave the ground floor.

An example of poor indirect lighting use would be putting lights between the first and second floor of a building. Yes, because the lights are over the players' heads they might not be able to directly see them, but lighting the second floor of a house is so unnatural that the players will not help but trace the light back to its source. A better way to illuminate the house would be with indirect lighting.

Direct

Direct lighting are accent lights that can be easily seen by players and so usually need a stronger justification for their placement, such as being lighting that would be expected in that world. The regular basement lights on the ceiling of a serial killer's basement would be noticeable if absent, and it wouldn't be surprising if the ancient city had torch lights illuminating the streets. This would solve the issue from direct lighting in the previous section: torches against the side of house would illuminate the upper section enough to convey the proper space of the environment. Sometimes the mood projected by direct lighting is worth breaking the story environment. A spotlight directly under an object can give it eerie shadows to project onto the wall that couldn't be replicated in any other way. A player will always forgive a technical limitation or two if it provides an overall more vibrant experience.

Direct lighting is especially great for highlighting the wayfinding points guiding players to puzzle interfaces, especially in ways that bring drama. For example, lights hanging from wires above puzzles can turn on one by one leading players down a hallway. This brings a unique animation to the room but also makes the room feel taller by drawing the eyes of the players towards the ceiling. A chandelier over a dining room table can turn on when players need to solve a paper puzzle, inviting them to draw together to solve it. In the haunted theater game, when it is time to move all the players into the theater, every light turns off in the room. Drawing them forward to the next location.

Prop

Prop lights are not just directly part of the game's reality but active in the story or puzzles of the game. As such they will always be clearly visual, prominently placed, and should have a direct backstory and a character explanation for their presence. This will either be from your characters needing a light source to accomplish their goals or because light is an active part of the puzzle being solved. For example, an explorer in an Egyptian tomb might set up several lights around the room set up by the archeologists in order to better record the hieroglyphics. If players were turning on a power generator as one of the room's puzzles then the power generator would need to display shining lights to confirm the puzzle is complete.

Direct lights work with prop lights in guiding player interaction. Prop lights, being in-game lighting, are only turned on by choices the players make. But direct lighting can be controlled by the game master to give the players stronger visual hints. For example, at one point of the haunted game, players turn on a small blinking spotlight that shows where they need to insert a crank. If they miss the subtle light they turned on, the game master has a control to direct them with a much larger spotlight that turns on and off at his discretion. The more players can interact with prop lighting in their room the better, however, so always consider if a certain puzzle can have more light elements or if there are additional lights that would have realistically been placed by your characters in the environment.

Reflections

Reflections from mirrors can add unique dimensions to game rooms and are a great way to double the usage of light and props and magnify the world. Using mirrors as accents for the room can greatly expand the space and add more interesting geometric patterns for the players. Would the room have mirrors as a common decoration? Would smoky mirrors give the feeling of dust and decay? Having some mirrors streaked with grease or dust give a greater sense of foreboding than much more expensive effects.

However, beware using eye level windows in prominent room positions. Strange reflections detract from the experience because they may highlight the everyday limitations of a room, such as wires, that would otherwise be invisible to players. If a mirror does not magnify the game environment from most angles, then its placement should be reconsidered. For example, the mirror might look great from most angles, but if players approach it from one particular side it will highlight the fire exit of the room. Better not to use it.

Transparency

Windows are another great, and cheap, way to expand your story environment. People love windows and will put them into any environment they wish to live in. Windows instantly convey if the world is friendly or hostile, rich or poor. There can be window displays of interiors to expand the sense of commerce of the world. There can be window displays of exteriors that hint of a larger world. A simple mural display on the edge of your room looks much more exciting through a window and, even better, the space between the window and the mural gives you the chance to add some simple lighting elements. Should a window be peered at through mysterious haze? Adding fog to the outside of your active game environment is as simple as it is spooky. How the world chooses to present itself always tells volumes about the welcoming (or unwelcoming) nature of the world.

Optical Illusions

Together, mirrors and windows are used to create some of the most popular optical illusions, so not only should their use in a room be considered, but common tricks that take advantage of their properties such as an infinite hallway or a pepper's ghost should be considered as well. Guests appreciate the chance to observe illusions even if they're not active parts of gameplay. However, many optical illusions are great chances to add easy observation puzzles that either welcome people into the unique style of the room at the beginning of the game or gain speed for the game's final sequences.

If you are planning on adding an optical illusion, though, make sure it is added early in the game's development. When we added a pepper's ghost to the haunted theater game we were limited in how long we could extend the sequence. We had built a platform for another part of the game and it would have been perfect to use the pepper's ghost in the platform but instead we had to settle for a less spectacular use of the effect. Sure, our players still jump more often than not, but I dream of what could have been. Ironically, the pepper's ghost haunts me.

Sound

There are three different ways sound is used in IPEs: as a soundscape, as music, and for puzzle sound effects. These directly correlate to the three light uses of direct, indirect, and prop: where each is closer and more directly controlled by the player. Each sound component has different considerations for the physical placement, volume, and frequency in order to best add to the game's atmosphere.

Soundscapes

Soundscapes are the sounds you would expect to hear in an environment simply by being there, even if the environment is fantasy. For example, if you were in a Victorian age you would expect to hear an occasional horse carriage moving along the road in a side street. If you were in a sci-fi environment you would expect the strange futuristic machines to quietly hum and randomly beep. If you were in a pirate ship you would expect to hear the quiet splash of water from the shoreline. Just like in landscaping, soundscaping is best appreciated when it takes the real and cultivates the presentation at multiple points. We want a garden with flowers, trees, and a lawn, but at spaces that help us appreciate each one. Similarly, We have an ideal placement for our sounds and IPEs let us live that expectation. We expect an occasional loud beep from the futuristic machine but would never want to be distracted by a loud wave washing against the beach.

Music

Music is the easiest way to give players their movie moments, as people love the idea of background music playing just for them as they perform heroic actions. Music doesn't have to be a full score right out of Disney Caribbean pirate ship, though, it can be simplified to a tune or even use natural sounds to more subtlety exist in the game. For example, "Alien" used a heartbeat that increased in agitation to promote fear before the alien attacked. While it was not a musical score, audiences were instinctively tense at the moments the "music" played. Music can also be used to introduce new areas or draw attention to specific events in the storyline of the game.

Music should not be so distracting as to pull the players from the experience and have them feel they are "pretending" to be other characters. For example, in a haunted game, playing the "ghostbusters" theme when the players aren't busting ghosts will make the room feel more like a themed party than an adventure. But playing "Mission Impossible" the exact moment players begin hacking a computer perfectly places them in the world of being a spy. Often inspiring music can be found searching the ASMR sections or "music to study to" sections of Youtube. A lot of great music work has already been done for you.

If the adventure naturally becomes more intense as the story progresses, then music can be used independently of the player's actions and controlled by the game master. If the game's threat increases as the timer ticks down, then it is only natural that the music becomes more exciting as the hour continues. Music can also change depending on how fast or slow players are solving the planned puzzles in a room. If a team is especially struggling, then music becomes a distraction. But a puzzle the players are excitedly solving becomes even better with a musical boost. I've had a few players tell me to turn down the music and that was definitely a design failure on my part: players should never really be conscious the music is there or the reasons why it might be changing.

To that end, always be careful when automating music into an experience. You're never quite sure when it is becoming frustrating to players and it is most likely to need to be adjusted on a team by team basis.

Sound Effects

Sound effects should be encountered when players are engaged with puzzles or the room's interactives, though we do sometimes have the game master activate them independently of the players to draw the player's attention. All electronic interfaces must have sound effects confirming correct player interaction because otherwise players will not know if they are successfully engaging the puzzle and will much more quickly give up on figuring out the puzzle than they will on its wooden equivalents.

To be more engaging, sound effects in puzzles could retain elements of the soundscape or music of the room. For example, sound effects can play parts of the room's theme song, like how in Disney's "Haunted Mansion" guests can hear the theme song in various surprising ways, from the organ, to a chorus, to even the wind. Sound layering also helps increase the organic feel of the environment. We've used some of the sound effects in our puzzles in the soundscape for our game and it has helped heighten the feeling of reality in the room.

Language

Language defines more of our interactions with the world than we think. From the frustration of seeing scribbled graffiti on our walls to the posted business hours we see before the shops we enter. The expression or absence of language tells players a lot about the attitudes of the people that live there. Makeshift or permanent, warnings or advertisements, each use of language portrays the attitudes of the land. Do they love rules? Do they love chaos? Are they romantic or utilitarian?

As many puzzles require some level of instruction to engage players, the shape of language used for hints can be especially important to establish. Be it a terrifying message left by past victims or an encouraging idea left by a friendly unicorn. There should always be a way to express hints without breaking the reality of the world. So taking the time to explore how language would work in your game without focusing on the game itself will very likely deepen your ability to express the world.

Smell

Smells can provide our most pervasive sense of a place. The smell of water, food, and steel inspires activity. The smell of decay and dust inspires concern. There are various ways to add smells to rooms, from complicated equipment to simple air fresheners. Froggy's Fog have a lot of scent additives for their fog machines that add instant mood enhancers. While it is difficult to keep a fog machine running during a game, letting it run for a moment during a game's reset will add a lingering scent to the room. We have DMX controllers that the Game master uses to provide the perfect amount of fog for each game.

The most important factor is to make sure your room does not smell like the everyday but has the subtle aura of being someplace special. Even a neutral smell can be engaging, such as the special clean smell of carefully maintained rides of Disney World, or the more rugged smell of gasoline among the rides in Six Flags. Let your players know this is an environment that is cared for in special ways.

Temperature

One important aspect to consider is the temperature of the room, as certain temperatures prompt certain expectations. Evaporation coolers can provide a noticeably unique temperature to the room, but even the basic chill of an air conditioner adds a clinical feel to a futuristic environment, or a slight heat creates the feel of a tropic jungle. As simple as one or two degrees outside the normal expected range is enough to give an impression of an otherworldly environment. While you want guests to be comfortable, slightly tweaking the physical environment amplifies the knowledge that they are in a "strange" world outside the ordinary.

Function & Potential Energy

We want to enter places that are an expression of power. Many of the most powerful machines we encounter display their potential energy through size alone. A sizeable puzzle interface has players wanting to tap the energy and potential of a machine and control the function.

A huge lever demands us to pull it and see what happens next. Potential energy in a IPE room, however, is best presented through illusions. Players do not need to control actual heavy equipment, so boxes full of materials can be empty, cases can house no electronics, and cooling systems can be strictly for show. The display of potential function can even misdirect players from the necessary functions of a room to run the show, such as counterweights, magnetic locks, A/C equipment, and security equipment.

A great expression of function is to show the illusion that gravity is being harnessed to its full ability. A stack of empty crates is easy to harness above the ground, but now your rigging seems to be holding hundreds of pounds instead of twenty at most.

Potential energy can also be expressed in the clear needs of a large number of people in an environment. A grocery store full of vegetables signals to the players that many people normally inhabit this environment. A lot of seating shows that this is a place that expects great groups of people.

Additionally, precarious stacking items on top of each other can demonstrate a dangerous or slapdash world. A stack of teacups piled sky high, while actually glued together, can provide the strong impression that they have been stacked randomly on a table and could topple over and break at any moment. This sense of nervous fragility provides a subtle yet exciting feel of dangerous and presence in the room.

When playing with this principle, however, make sure that the illusion cannot be broken by players. If they can easily interact with objects that should be heavy but are instead light, then the environment will lose a large sense of reality. If their placement looks gratuitous and unnatural in the environment then it is doubly jarring because large objects really stand out. I created a large turbine in one of my games but wasn't able to fit it into the environment as well as it should so its placement seems more odd than exciting. It feels like it could be easily removed without making a strong difference to the world. Removing huge pieces from your environment should create the impression that essential elements are missing. While a large air conditioning machine is right next to every major building, the majority of people wouldn't notice its absence. But a shipping yard without crates to ship? That feels empty.

Cultural Expectation

Potential energy is the expression of the machines to make an environment run, but the human element can be just as expressive in an environment and more important to providing a place with meaning. Imagine going to a beach wedding. Since the entire point is to be next to the ocean there shouldn't be anything more than the bride and groom, right? And yet you've probably imagined the usual archway, some flower decorations, benches, and carpet leading up to the archway. That's because the idea of a special place for the bride and groom to stand is too deeply ingrained into the cultural expression of a wedding. But good news: place that archway, basic flowers, seating, and rolling rug in an empty room and you could instantly throw a "wedding" escape game.

And the more we cover cultural expectations in an environment the more it feels like a real place. Add a reception hall and a vestibule to your wedding escape game and players will really feel they are in a place prepared by people that they need to search and understand. Covering every cultural consideration of a room helps it feel bigger than life.

While the "Tower of Terror" in Disney World could just be elevators in a basement, it is the journey through a completely designed hotel that makes it feel special. From wandering the gardens to the lobby: you really feel that you are part of a true hotel by seeing the warm lighting, fireplace, flowers, and inspiring sculptures among the dust and spiderwebs.

Skeuomorphism

And you thought these elements wouldn't get weird! Skeuomorphism is most often used in online graphic user interface design to create elements that help better conceptualize their concepts by mimicking elements of their real-world counterparts. The most well-known example is the recycle bin icon used for discarding files that you see on your computer screen. The bin gives a clear understanding of where the files will go and what their ultimate fate will be. If the icon was just an "X" you wouldn't feel right using it because "X" gives the feeling that you shouldn't go that way. The function would be exactly the same but people would be storing their files in "delete" folders instead of using the actual delete function. Why? Because people like the skeuomorphic concepts of folders. Remember, there are computer purists that miss the days of DOS and hate that we'd rather have irrelevant sunsets or cute offspring staring at our faces instead of the comforting black void and blinking white prompts that is the truth of computer work.

So it is important when your puzzle requires turning on fake candles that you mimic the reality as closely as possible, like "using" an actual lighter with a magnet glued to the end to light each candle as you "tap" it. Using a lighter instead of pressing a button makes the electronic moment more real. This added component helps bridge the reality gap because it adds more elements of how true candles work to the process of playing the puzzle.

Besides adding dynamics to the gameplay, skeuomorphism can also make the room more visually fun for players as they interact with additional gameplay components. For example, adding fake "heat sink" elements or bolts to your machines helps the players feel more like those machines are made of steel than wood and plastic. You can also add fake elements of decay, like cracks and cobwebs, that make the place feel more ancient.

Animation

Animation in your room is any gratuitous movement. Not every room has a cause for animation, after all a lot of places with puzzles in them are foreboding because they are so still, but if a room could benefit from animation it should be strongly considered, especially because you rarely need more than one animated effect per room.

Anything that can't be controlled by the staff or the players but instead simply exists in the environment will keep the room from feeling like a stage and more a true place. When you step into a backyard you seeing the clouds moving above you and the water bubbling in a stream below, elements that cannot be controlled by the gardener. You know you are in a place that has the raw elements of the natural and the unexpected in it.

Animation can be added using a various number of techniques, from a carefully maintained water feature, to shifting light, to using fans to create subtle air currents that can swing ropes and curtains. Fog can roll down from on high, machinery can spin, a snow machine can give bursts of snow, and even an occasional wave of bubbles can burst into the room. Animation can be especially useful to add to the top layers of your environment, such as the satin curtains simulating fire on the higher level of the set of the Pirates of the Caribbean in Disney World. You don't have to break your budget on creating an animated element: anything that can cap off the corner or ceiling of your room will do. Disney's Hollywood Studios installed a traffic sign that constantly switched between "STOP" and "GO." Following their example, installing a traffic light that switches between red, yellow, and green in the corner of your room costs barely any money but now makes your "alley" set feel exciting and real.

Illusions

Illusions are the magic tricks in the room. Like animation, you don't need a lot and you don't need to break the bank using them, but even having just one will make the experience incredibly more special. The rule is simple: put more effort into the trick then the audience would ever expect. In the Indiana Jones ride in Disney, at one moment it looks like a giant boulder is rolling towards you. However, your jeep, the room, and an Indiana Jones suspended from a rope are all moving towards a static boulder. It was not actually all that more expensive than any of the other rooms in the ride, but it looked fantastically so. Anything that you can accomplish that adds just a bit more to your budget and reset time, like fake wall that can fall away to reveal a clue inside, should strongly be considered.

There is no limit to what can be used in illusions effects. Audio, lighting, complimentary colors, reflections, transparencies, video, all of these and more can be combined to create tricks of all shapes and sizes. The best part is that even if the audience is familiar with the mechanics of the tricks used they'll still love the feeling of control that comes from having their own private show in an IPE. The magic trick finales in rooms I've used have almost never been examined by the players. When you go to a magic show, the challenge is figuring out how the trick is solved so that's what you focus on: a battle of wits with your magician. When you are at a puzzle room, though, you are battling puzzles so you're willing to give magic tricks a break and just consider them magic.

Interactives

No matter how much you love an activity, you'll occasionally want a quick break from the action to catch your breath. In sports, it's a drink of water. In IPEs, it is interactives: items that can clearly be interacted with but are not puzzles. Most commonly, these are simple toys, works of art, or costumes. Interactives help you enjoy the environment simply as an identity-rich place.

Museums started as places simply to enjoy artwork, but as they evolved the breaks from art became as important as the art itself. People wanted benches to rest on, audio visual guides to listen to, and cafes to eat in. IPEs rarely last long enough for people to desire snacks or drinks, but there are still plenty of companies that incorporate that into the experience. When we stop for a snack, we clear our minds and better prepare ourselves for our next experience. And for those that find the main experience hard to grasp, such as younger or less engaged players, interactives are the perfect time fillers while everyone else solves complicated puzzles. Younger players can come back to the main game when the next big moment is about to begin.

Interactives can be easy puzzles, toys, extra design elements, or ways to earn in-game clues. They can be devices such as bells, instruments, buttons, cameras, guns, joysticks, levers, lights, pumps, spinning wheels, steering wheels, and touchscreens. They can even be small tasks that have been clearly set aside from the game area, such as playing with stickers, making masks, simple jigsaw puzzles, coloring, or stamps.

Interactives can also be the most animated parts of game mechanics in the puzzles themselves. The chance to blast air, spray water, or trigger movements is absorbing to all ages. Interactives can even trigger story backgrounds: moments that clearly are not clues in the game but help players appreciate the richness of their environment. For example, players can play with a model train in a Victorian set. While the model train can be used to solve a puzzle, continuing to play with it after the puzzle is solved would be fun because model trains are fun. In room design it's always important to stop and ask: what would I want to play with if I were just spending time here and not on a mission to be a champion?

Just make sure that interactives are clearly separate from the gameplay as much as possible. If interactives are given too much of a spotlight then players will begin to assume they are puzzle elements. They should always be in separate boxes, on pegs, or to the side of the main action in a room. The more they feel like clear "play time" to the players the better. Rubber swords and shields hung up on the wall are clear to players that they could take them down to sword fight but don't necessarily have to. A sword that is pulled from the stone, only to end up being a fun prop, is confusing. Interactives should also be less detailed and, in general, just feel less special than the props being used for puzzles. A block with mysterious symbols on it will always draw a puzzle player more than just an alphabet block.

Physicality

Physicality is the attention to the contact or feel of the room, such as the textures, structures, and the dimensions of the transitions (how the doors or walls physically swing open). Physicality helps players make decisions more than they realize. When we enter a new room we do not just enter a place of functions but feelings, with a shift in the flooring from carpet, wood, bricks, or tile. And since IPEs almost always take place inside it is even more important to stretch physicality. Stepping onto artificial grass is not an expensive effect but makes a world of difference to players. Basically, we appreciate change the most when it hits all of our senses: when we feel a different texture under our feet, ascend to a new height, and enter a new atmosphere.

Physicality can be used with ramps, carpet, stone paths, wood bridges, and so on. Physicality can even be subtly used, like having players step onto a layer of wooden boards on the floor (the simple height difference will feel like a transition) or walk through an air curtain. Anything that has players think they are walking "through" or "onto" something is an expression of this element. Physicality can be as simple as two rows of rocks on the floor. Paths can usually be differentiated by rocks so players will instinctually separate the room into two places: on the left of the rock path and on the right of the rock path. And if the rock path leads to and from places then players will try to understand why that path was made. Buying Landscape rocks from overstock.com is all it takes to immediately make your room more interesting.

Destruction and danger are also great ways to add immediate physicality to an environment. By having destroyed elements in the room, such as broken statues or chandeliers, players will immediately know they are in a place beyond control. Destruction is most often caused by nature in human environments, so a few vines or a large rock on the players path is enough to convey a robust (and dangerous) natural presence in the room.

Physicality invites danger by giving us drop offs and ledges that are not expected in comfortable environments. You can fake a ledge simply by having a fence over an area that is painted black. Players will know not to cross the fence because to do so is "dangerous."

Physicality also invites us to interact with an environment by showing us items that invite touching, such as especially large buttons or mysterious holes. It is best to have any pushable button connected to an interactive, though, so that people can see the controlled kinetics and not just press buttons that do nothing. But given the choice between having buttons that do nothing and no buttons at all, use buttons.

Pace/Intensity

The intensity of a room is controlled by how often something happens. Faster music, more flashing lights, and more animation: each encourage actions and reactions from the players. While most of the room's energy will come from how the players choose to engage it, the intensity can also be increased at certain designated times (like the halfway mark) or by certain actions the players chose to make, like entering a new area. Intensity can also be controlled by more unique situations, such as interacting with characters, if the players are taking "good" or "evil" actions, or if the setting is fantasy or horror. However, you do not want so many intense "events" that players get overwhelmed or no longer feel like the heroes in their environment. A good example of an environmental factor to add would be a thunderstorm: it naturally would increase during the course of the game but players wouldn't feel like they were expected to be "in control" of it.

In-betweens

In animated movies, there is always the key art and the in-betweens. Key art expresses the most important elements, but without the in-betweens there is never the breath of life that connects all the moments. In-betweens make art become alive.

This is because there is a difference between the essential and majestic. Key art shows us all the points of a story. The characters snap into pose after pose. You can understand a film by flipping through the key art but it would be unsatisfying artistically because no extra effort has been put into the work. The in-betweens are the time and energy that helps people appreciate the product, even if it isn't naturally to their liking. With the in-betweens comes motion, color, and music. You appreciate a seven-tier wedding cake even if it's not your favorite flavor, for the craftmanship and size alone.

If in a room all the artwork and design elements are geared around the puzzles alone than the place will not feel real because we never enter a place filled to brim with puzzles and nothing else. Imagine a room built specifically to display jigsaw puzzles. You would find it lackluster if it was a bunch of small plastic tables containing puzzles. Yes, the puzzles would be displayed, but not well and not with effort. A true display room would still have display cases to protect the puzzles, special lighting to showcase them, and posted guides and illustrations explaining the history of the puzzles to make the experience special. You can buy an engagement ring out of a cardboard box, but would you want to? So even our expectations of "neutral spaces" have details and efforts that need to be filled in if it is going to meet our expectations on an experience.

A secret, abandoned temple deep in a forest would have evidence that animals and people had been there. A serial killer wouldn't just have a stash of weapons in his lair but cleaning supplies to cover his tracks, evidence from his victims, and tracking equipment to spy on the authorities after him. A pirate ship wouldn't just have maps on tables and treasures in chests but provisions for a long journey, tools for sailing, and weapons for fighting. It would be anchored in a harbor or wrecked on a beach.

In-betweens expand the world of every individual puzzle. If the puzzle was to enter a haunted house, then the solution might be accessing a key hidden beneath the front porch's floorboards. One false board can be lifted to reveal a key stashed underneath. That's the key art. But the board can wobble when stepped on to draw attention to it. There can be a welcome mat that needs to be removed to access the board. You can place a swing on the porch and a knocker on the door as interactives, lights on the porch for color, even dirt beneath the floorboard for smell. All these are the in-betweens that make the environment feel real and exciting. The puzzle dynamic is ultimately the same, but now the world has many moments beyond the simple moment of "how to get inside the house."

There are many ways to get into an "in-betweens" mindset. One of the best is to consider sounds. When we step into a new environment the first thing we note is the different sounds. Disney world uses lots of sound barriers. Pandora in Animal Kingdom has guests step across a bridge that has sounds of strange chirping insects on either side. While the physical bridge would be enough to signify the new area, the wave of sound you pass by really makes you feel that you are someplace entirely new. If a place doesn't meet the sound expectations then people will not feel a part of the world. With the sounds, however, are the objects that make the sounds. Bringing them physically into the world will heighten the experience. For example, we expect to hear creepy music in a haunted house. Adding a gramophone that can play the music is a great way to heighten the experience as well as possibly add a new fun puzzle.

In-betweens can also sometimes go beyond sound effects and add entire side-conversations to an environment. Nothing makes a place feel more authentic than hearing a secret conversation taking place around the corner by unseen people. As people will want to be engaged in puzzles this should be a clearly gratuitous, but the occasional snippet of an argument from the just-out-of-sight fish market in Victorian England makes the players feel like they are in a real world.

A great in-between to add is encroaching nature, especially in older environments. Players can see crumbling walls, vines poking through the floor, and other elements of decay throughout the world. How nature reclaims a space is the greatest expression of the lost human element and inspires the possibility of uncovering long abandoned secrets. What is peeking through the cracks of the world?

Signage is a great in-between, as most of the places we go to have unique labels, instructions, and numbering. Especially when associated with travel. Signage is also the greatest clue language to add to an environment as we use signs to learn about how to exist in strange environments. Many IPE scenarios are in high trafficked areas, so signage can be an especially useful, as well as adding the safety elements and crowd control elements that we often overlook in our initial planning but feel "missing" when we enter environments without their additions. For example, what is a grocery store without a row of carts for other people? Or what is an apartment building without a fire escape? Even adding a simple ladder or a single shopping cart is enough to make an environment feel more real.

The idea of being "in between" can be literal. When exploring places we love to look between the cracks and see what we're not meant to see. The connections between train cars have gaps that passengers can look through to see the earth rolling beneath them. A single gratuitous window showing a ladder in the distance tells a story beyond the established world and makes the entire world richer.

Perhaps the most important in-between to use is art. Almost all puzzle environments are set in places where art would be promoted and displayed. If we are in a mansion or theater then we expect to see art there that expresses the spirit of the place. Does the art want to welcome us, showcase aspects of a character's personality, or threaten us? Art can even reveal subtle aspects of character. Is the art decorative or mechanically clever? Does it bring objects to the environment or use objects already found there? For example, does the Victorian mansion stick to English art in the rooms or is there a Chinese or Italian themed room?

Even greater than art (and a stronger impression to players) is the expression found in gardens and plants. There is something powerful about the idea of controlled nature, and the strong human presence behind its maintenance in an environment. The attempt to nurture life even foreboding places is also very distinctly human. Any expression of plants in your environment should be pursued.

It's also good to remember that the most common use of art we see is advertisements. There can be "window shopping" displays in your environment. Many places we inhabit try to be fancy to make us buy something or impress us with the importance of the people who live and work there. Your environment should indulge in this rule of human nature and not ignore it. Window shopping is especially good for prop displays because it doesn't carry the expectation of actually purchasing the wares and so players will feel less pressure to inspect and explore it.

However there are also places in which art would not be expected. Places of abandonment, decay, industrial function or natural purity. These are the places where we focus simply on function. The important thing is to make sure that your in-betweens highlight the most logical function that would exist in the environment. The absence of art should have a clear reason why it does not exist: a place of abandoned decay (rust and dust), industry (machines and supplies), or nature (trees and water). Any of these locations either exist solely for production or have no people present to hang art. If art should not exist in your environment it should be very clear to you why.

While exploring all these in-between possibilities, it is important to ensure that all in-betweens enhance the "key art" of an experience. A creepy, abandoned theater should have creepy in-betweens and not cute ones. You aren't trying to cram truly gratuitous, random details into your would or make it so multi-dimension that it truly could operate as a real place. You want enough details to fill the peripheral vision of your players and not overwhelm their focus. For example, if you have a dragon cave filled with treasures then a great in-between would be to have a throne among the treasures to help give the idea that he raided a medieval kingdom. To also include the treasures of medieval tapestries would overwhelm the player. Showing the roasted armor of a knight invites the idea of previous battles the dragon has faced. Showing the knight's squire dead too brings too much attention to the experience.

Continuation

Continuation is expressed when elements naturally continue past your ability to see them. Fantasy books chart out complete maps of their worlds that always include places that the characters won't visit, but it makes the world feel more complete to see an entire map of the world and inspires the imagination of the players.

Windows and doors are the most classic elements used in continuation. These are the false portals that make it seem like we are in a larger environment. In Disney World's Haunted Mansion ride, we drift past many doors, making the mansion feel like it could truly fit

999 ghosts while still having room for one more. However, in theme parks we don't mind passing locked doors we encounter because we are riding and not exploring the environment. In IPE games it is very important that a false portal never give the impression that it will soon be opened by the players. The best false portals are on second floors, behind fences without gates, across a foliage divide, or through permanent windows. We enjoy seeing other functions laid out in windows that the adventure will not require, such as dining or shopping. But we do not want to feel that we are missing out.

For example, if we came across a village full of mushroom huts we wouldn't mind seeing huts of all shapes and sizes if we knew we were entering enough huts to get a full understanding of the village. But we wouldn't want to miss the blacksmith hut or the mayor's mansion hut. Players want the best of the environment.

A fence is also a great way to use continuation in your environment as players can see elements beyond it, such as flowers and fields. You can also use fences to give players items they can reach for between the bars and even touch, though they cannot actively play with them, such as statues. In rooms, it is great to have at least one fake wall to take advantage of adding windows, doors, or fences to the room.

Destruction can also be used to create continuation in a room, such as having stairs to an upper level that is now inaccessible because it has fallen apart. Stones in pathways can also be great natural blocks in the environments. Players won't interact with a blank wall but instead inaccessible portals to the rest of the world.

Adding second levels to environments is also great for continuation. Players can see a tower over their heads that is naturally separated from them by a stone wall and feel they are in a much deeper environment. Or players can see the same fence but shrunk on the second level. The second level is also a great chance to add additional false portals to the environment.

Interruption

Interruption is the physical excitement of stumbling into an action already in progress. When we discover a murder scene we immediately feel the ramifications of the great actions that have taken place: the spilled coffee, the bloody knife, the crumpled body. It is the knowledge that we must find the murderer as quickly as possible that drives us to immediately search for clues. His actions being interrupted by us immediately make us the hero of the story and the one chance to get justice for the victim.

A disaster area is a place interrupted by the shock and power of nature, so when we enter it we immediately want to jump into stabilizing the damage and making repairs. Jumping into a story provides more immediate excitement and puzzle cues.

Continuation zooms out on to the wider world, but interruption zooms into the world's details. The more players feel like they're trespassing on a private moment, the better the use of interruption expression. Players should have a feel for exactly the type of characters that were just using the props and that by trespassing on their usage they have a unique chance to understand what is going on. For example, an interrupted card game (with one player having an extra card in his hand) is a great way to show the character's lives and who is secretly a scoundrel.

Places of high traffic are perpetually full of interrupted action, so the idea of luggage, documentation, and even half-eaten sandwiches gives the sense that others could return any second to pick it back up. We would also expect a post-office to be full of items in various states of process: being sent in, being examined, and being sent out. Both work and play can be interrupted.

Another element of interruption is the "half completed" task. Cleaning is needed in every environment that people live in, so it is one of the most common interruptions that can be discovered. If we see clothes drying we know that the person is in the process of cleaning and will soon return to the task, but it makes sense that they have wondered off at the moment to do something else. It is exciting to interrupt the progression of a task that will soon be concluding. When you enter a kitchen and see that the coffee pot is brewing a cup you know that someone will very soon be returning.

Pinballing

Pinballing is the deliberate positioning of conditions that cause players to bounce from one area to another. A pinball game uses wild colors, ramps, and lights so that it is always exciting to watch the pinball bounce around the board. Striking the different sections expresses different functions and causes greater contrasts in the game. The greater the contrast, the more fun the pinballing.

Similarly, sections of IPE rooms should be distinct with different shapes, colors, and functions. A fluid blue fish should be found in a crude, rough box. Even the same object can be contrasted. A map can be framed and orderly (created by an adult) or massive and sloppy (created by a child). Contrasts draw the eye to the form.

Pinballing can also be used to enhance more metaphorical expression as well. For example, the standard ideas of masculine and feminine can be displayed in the room by having darker colors contrasted to lighter ones.

Pinballing is also a commonly seen expression in nature, either through the contrasts of plants and trees or between man-made structures and natural structures. Anything that displays different ideas of beauty or uses of structure can be perfect for pinballing effects.

The chief use of pinballing is to remove the possibility of bland uniformity in an environment. Without different sections or juxtaposed forms, people lose interest. More importantly, because puzzle interfaces are themselves unique, if they are presented in a uniform environment they become strange. Puzzles would more naturally be at home in a place with pinballing elements.

Placemaking

Placemaking is deliberately feeding multiple pathways to a certain icon or point to make a place that clearly stands out to the players. The main reason to feed pathways to this place is to offer furniture for resting and more intense visual delights. Statues and fountains at parks always have multiple paths leading to them and seating options around them. Placemaking points in rooms can also accommodate tables for solving puzzles and more neutral lighting for examining puzzle components. The need of a place to rest and examine is strong enough that people will often make places if none have been provided and they will lean against railings, sit on steps, or even sit on tables. And if there is no place to examine puzzles, people will lay them onto the floor to review them. While placemaking is not the most important element of a room, it should always be considered. If a sofa can exist in your environment be sure to add it.

Subdivision

Subdivisions are obstacles in pathways that create extraneous movements when players need to walk around them. Living Rooms will have sofas in the middle of the room to delineate the space into separate sections. Boundaries help people establish order in their minds. For example, hedges in gardens help guide people through the garden highlights and ensure people see every section. Subdivisions can also come from unnatural elements in the environment, like the temporary blocked path from construction items or traffic management.

By inviting extraneous movement in the environment, subdivisions add to the feeling of discovery as players follow the divisions from one site to another and by making people work harder to reach items it makes the items themselves more interesting. If you can only reach an item by stepping around obstacles in your path you will want it more.

Stratification

Stratification is the basic principle behind the beauty of mountains: different layers build upon each other to make the whole more impressive than the parts. A natural example of stratification is the pools of water that make up a waterfall. As the water cascades down, every level is comprised of fundamentally the same elements (water and rocks) but the way the water playfully hits the rocks and pools in the stream makes it an intriguing landscape.

Additional layers beyond the active level of players automatically deepens the world. We use higher levels to display art that we want to keep out of reach or for storing items that we do not need every day. So stratification tells us that there is more to the universe then what we will immediately be experiencing.

However, it should always be clear that not reaching these additional layers doesn't make players feel they are losing out on an experience. The stratification layers need to either be continuations of what they can already access during the course of the game, such as rooms of the same general nature, or larger than life elements that they would need to tackle in a completely new adventure, like a mountain, completely new town, or castle.

For example, if players enter one cottage during the course of the game, then having additional cottages out of reach due to stratification will not bother the players. But if players see an extravagant, mysterious mansions towering above them, it will be disappointing if they never reach it. Only if the game's adventure becomes more exciting than a mansion, like, for example, they enter the cottage so that they can access the fairy woods where fantastic feats of magic await them, does the games stratification remain balanced.

As a good rule, no puzzle element should be more than five feet tall so that they can be reached and completely seen by all guests. As the typical room is about a total of 8 feet high, this gives three feet in every room that can be used for stratification decorations, including vines in the ceiling, murals on the tops of walls, and unique lighting fixtures. Lights are especially good at stratifying spaces, either with poles or highlighting mysterious out-of-reach rooms.

Horizontal stratification is possible as well, though usually must be accomplished through video screens. Watching scenery go by from a train window gives the impression that you are truly moving along the train line. Or, by having grids in your environment, players can feel they are making a longer journey than they are. For example, having girders in your mine shaft makes the mine shaft feel longer than if the walls were smooth.

Be careful that the stratification elements in a room never overwhelm the puzzles. If the designs are too intricate or detailed then the puzzles shrink in importance. I once was in a fairy tale room that had so many fantastic elements in the ceiling of the room that it was disappointing playing with the teapots and blocks below.

Forced Perspective

If you're looking to do really advanced creative work in your room then forced perspective is the choice for you. Forced perspective is about deliberately creating angles that aren't about their practicality but about drawing the viewer's eye. They can be an idealized reality that help us better process a space.

The grounds of the graveyard can look larger when the graves in the upper section are half the size of the graves in the lower. And having buildings bend towards you can give you a fantastic paranoid feel, like all the buildings have been squeezed together to stare down at you. IPEs are an excellent place for forced perspective because they do not have to conform to the practicalities of the real world. A towering castle so imposing that it literally leans over you is impractical if people needed to truly live in it, but it can be whatever shape it needs to be if its only function is to intimidate the players.

Negative Space

Negative space is space deliberately kept neutral so as not to overwhelm players with options and choices. I feel after describing all the different ways you can fill your room with objects the least I can do is give you a break, right? Well, the same is true for your players. Negative space is a clear break from the action and great for delineating other elements of expression. A neutral area around a statue calls greater attention to the details of the statue by having nothing distracting around it. A lot of puzzles also benefit from having negative space padding around them, especially so that other players can easily see the puzzle's action and offer suggestions on how to proceed. The presentation of water (which can be just painted onto the floor) is one of the best negative space materials because we are used to seeing large expanses of water unadorned with objects. But it can also be useful to have seating sections with carpet displays. We never want our intricate carpets to be missed so we typically won't put too many items on them.

UNLOCKING AN IDEAL ENVIRONMENT

There are a lot of ways to organize your game and what works for my company may not necessarily work for you. The last thing I'm looking for in an industry this young is a "one size fits all" idea of corporate engagement. We're just beginning to figure out how to have fun mobile IPE games, in home IPE games, and bed and breakfast IPE games after all. Imagine getting a murdered heiress with your scrambled eggs!

But I have seen way too many Escape Room set up a "standard" corporate feel for their rooms which strikes me as... well. When you go to the dentist that corporate feel makes sense to me. You want the people operating on your teeth as professional and credentialed as possible. Now when you go to a putt-putt game, a bowling alley, or a theme park just how many "Teamwork makes the dream work!" posters, waiver signing stations, or corporate jargon speeches do you really expect to endure? So when reading this chapter just ask yourself, "are my customers more likely to enjoy exciting novelty or proper oral hygiene?" and plan accordingly!

Exterior Game Environments

Before players begin to play the game, they will encounter the world's entrance. The entrance of the world should be as carefully crafted as the world they explore. Each element they encounter should prepare them for what they can expect from the experience. This goes beyond the marketing they view when purchasing the game to all the live elements: the building they enter and the staff they meet. It is crucial that these moments build towards the reality that they are about to become heroes in the game itself.

Lobby

The Lobby encompasses all the out-of-game discussions and activities (ticket sales, merchandise sales, bathroom breaks, snack purchases) while still maintaining the reality of the game as much as possible. The lobby can still have hints about the game space, but most hints should be a part of the pre-show. After all, most lobbies will lead to multiple game worlds and so players aren't really in "game mode" yet. Instead, it is better for the lobby to contain queue media, such as videos that explain the backstory of the world or general trailers showing what the world is like. Online you don't want trailers longer than thirty seconds so, now that they are here, you can show them the two minute long original take of the trailer. Players will already start to feel like they are more special when they see the "extended cut" of the media that is only available on-site. Like all queue media, it should not be necessary for playing the game, but instead fun additions that make the world feel more rich.

Inevitably, there will be some players that need to wait in the lobby pre or post game. Occupied time always feels shorter than unoccupied time so additional amenities for guests are always appreciated. The lobby should provide all the common expectations of comfort and relaxation to players, from seating, to watching, to toys. Especially toys. It is also a good time to talk to the staff about subjects outside of the game experience, such as restaurant or other IPE game recommendations.

One of the most effective lobbies I've seen had rich, brown leather couches and a large video screen displaying their game trailers. The owner was clearly proud of his work and wanted players to hang out and enjoy his location outside of playing games. People could relax, explore more products, or talk about the games: a perfect lobby experience. His games were good but not amazing. And I would return to his room with a group of friends just because of his lobby alone. I know the lobby would make them feel special so I'd trust any game he provided for my team. That's the standard.

Pre-show

The first thing the audience sees on a stage is never the show itself but always the curtain separates the everyday of our lives from the magic of some place special. When we watch other people perform the curtain is pulled back for us, but when we are the performers, we can push back the curtain.

The "curtain" doesn't have to be fabric, though. As modern playhouses have taught us, the space before a play begins can be a black box or reality "on pause." Escape game companies have their pre-show be specially decorated doors that players step through before entering the world, neutral areas where they play introductory media for the room, or the first room itself but with a game host explaining the rules before the game begins. Each of these approaches can be best depending on the building, game, and storyline. So it's important to consider the special pre-show elements when making your decision.

The pre-show area has an element of exploration to it because players are now trying to learn about the game and what it will be truly like.

They are right up against the physical reality of the game, but they are not yet able to interact with any puzzles (even if it is just because the game host is still there and it would be awkward to do so) and the count-down clock is not active. Basically, players can explore but not progress. Pre show areas can accommodate all the elements of expression, but especially the interactives. We store masquerade masks in our pre-show area that are used for the photo opportunities at the end of the game.

The pre-show has the most important and final explanation of how the world works. This will always include the explanations of how the puzzles in the world actually work, such as explaining any locks used in the world. Supplies and tools for the games can be given here, especially tools that are extraneous to solving individual puzzles, such as flashlights or a portable hint/objective system. Players should know they are fully prepped to play the game as soon as the curtain parts.

Lobby Host

The lobby host will always meet the players in the lobby and help them prepare for the game. This is the best time to give the players general supplies they need for the game, such as flashlights or white boards for taking notes. Whatever the lobby host introduces should be useful but not integral to solving a puzzle. It is very hard for players to separate their everyday items from the game items. Believe me, I know. In one of my games I gave them flashlights that they later use to uncover a secret in a wall. It does not work well because people have a very difficult time organically connecting the dots and I almost always have to explain the concept again to them.

The lobby host should always be the person introducing the player to the limitations of the room. If there are plugs that shouldn't be messed with, now is the time to tell them. If there's a real fire exit in the room that has confused players before, warn them now. People get that some rooms have limitations in their budgets. As long as the puzzles are fun (and the price reflects the limitations) then they are still excited about the experience.

But never tell them about the limitations of the environment inside of the room. First off, it immediately lowers the excitement of the game. When you're standing on top of a volcano rattling off that the lava isn't real you sure aren't making me excited to hunt for virgin sacrifices. If your group is going to be receptive to warnings, they'll be receptive wherever you tell them. If they aren't then you're going to need to give them an in-game warning no matter the case. And if you don't trust people in your rooms at all so you want to give them as many lectures, warnings, and stickers as possible: you are in the wrong business. Seriously. The companies I've known with that attitude have already gone out of business.

Game Host

The game host always talks to the players in the pre-show area. He can retrieve them from the lobby or meet them exclusively in the game host area, depending on the story. A wizard entering the lobby, for example, to fetch the players to a magical world is a fun way to start the game. A common servant in a haunted mansion, however, would probably be more fun to first see inside of the room. So a good first question is how much power the game host has in the world. Is he the most powerful character the players will meet, or is he the least powerful? In my show, while I great people as a ghost host that knows a lot about the history of the theater, it is the spirits that are truly in charge and so I constantly call out to them.

The game host can either help players out with preparations for the game or entirely be in character. There are many games that will have the game host be a video introduction, a character's audio clips, or a letter of greeting the players can read themselves. Whatever the case, the game host should never have to break character.

He may or may not be a mentor figure of the world. If he comes to "fetch" the players for their assistance then they are immediately drawn into the world. If he prepares them and accompanies players into the universe. He accompanies the players into the universe and will help them exit from the game, either by congratulating them on their success or helping them solve any remaining puzzles. Depending on the game, he can stay in the world to guide the players or enter and exit the world over the threshold. Like any mentor character that can travel between the fantastic and the ordinary, he should be able to perform any needs in the real world, but should not break character while doing so. For instance, if the game host comes from a fantasy environment, then a comment about the strangeness of the "portal devices" when handing players a smart tablet would be a good way to remain in character.

If a room does not have a game host then the game master will take over their duties. However, this is usually not the best choice because, should the players lose or the game malfunction for any reason, the game host will have to enter the room out-of-character. I was once playing a prison game where we were stuck in jail cells. Every time we had to ask for help the game master would come into the room and give us clues. It really broke the illusion that we were escaping a prison when the "jailer" could waltz into the room at any time and check on our progress. Similarly, having a game master escort you through the final puzzles once your time runs out really limits the power of your world and cheapens the story the players are experiencing. If you are limited in your staff choices, then the best idea is typically an audio cue that plays at the beginning and end that is activated by the game master. Having video is more difficult to incorporate because it can never be a cooler experience than that of the players and it should not rob the environment of its importance by having a "corporate feel to it." But a disembodied voice explaining the premise along with a music track is almost always going to be more fun for players. The feel of living a radio play brings more imagination to it than simply watching something on a screen.

Again, the best creative decision is the one that fits your environment. A disembodied voice in a spy game? Of course a video screen is more technological and cool. The Simpsons ride in Universal Studio without seeing the Simpsons animated? You feel robbed of really being in the show. But how many queue lines have had video presentations that are more frustrating than fun as they slow you down with characters you don't care about explaining a situation you're not interested in? And think of how many queue lines that are more exciting when you hear "Emergency! Please proceed down the hall as quickly as possible" in the background or hear the disembodied voice of the "ghost host" in the Haunted Mansion? There will always be a game better suited for a live actor, a video recording, or an audio clip. The most important factor remains that the game host does not break character when giving players their game experience.

Game Master

The Game Master is the most absolutely essential of all the roles because he makes sure the player's games actually runs as it is supposed to. He watches the players through the game's surveillance equipment as well as the game's HMI interface (should it have one). His main job is to run the game's equipment, including all music cues, light cues, sound cues, and special effects, as well as providing the players the hints they need to solve at least 90% of the game before the hour is up. The Game Master is also in charge of the physical pre-game set-up and post-game reset and gives the green light for the next game to begin. He can also perform minor repairs between games. It's more fun to have an ambitious game that needs low-level maintenance than an unambitious game that constantly runs smoothly, after all. If your players never have the freedom to do something wrong (and then be corrected as necessary by the game master) than you're missing something essentially fun about IPEs.

Energy Control

The energy goal of a successful game is well known. When your players say, "Wow, that felt like five minutes!" you know they've had a great time. But wow have I been in some rooms that have trusted their deadly energy. I've walking from one confusing puzzle element to another, trusting they'll eventually make sense to me. One minute becomes five becomes ten until I'm finally ready to ask the game master for a hint. And the hint? If it's a confusing multi-sentence mess well, at that point I really get the "Escape" adjective because I want to be anywhere else.

Before I worked in puzzle design, I wrote and edited professional scripts. And I got really great at reading potential scripts and knowing when they would never pick up in energy. There's a point when you know the cliches are going to keep coming and coming and the script is never going to get better. If you don't even have any crumbs of intrigue in the very first page then by the time you get to the exploding server room and the triple double cross you just want to be done. Seriously. If the first lines of dialogue wouldn't even pass as interested in a bead store, then I know the rest of the script will be terrible. The same is true for rooms. A room that doesn't plan its energy well is never going to pick up in the final moments and present a fantastic puzzle. It'll just remain really disappointing throughout the experience. If you're lucky the players will just hate your room. If you're unlucky the players will also hate each other. So how do you know for sure that the room has deadly energy?

First off, every group will have a unique energy to bring to the game and experienced game masters and game hosts will know it. Some players appreciate being given a constant stream of hints and some prefer the chance to struggle and think things out themselves. You'll be able to figure out which group is which quickly, because a group that loves a struggle will bring clear energies to the experience that other groups will not. They'll be writing down clues that aren't clues and asking questions about elements of the room before you've even unleashed them on a puzzle. They'll experiment with their hands and talk to each other. They'll also organize themselves into teams and have some people searching while other people immediately hop onto the most accessible puzzle.

A group that is less engaged will either be overly nervous about the experience in general or will all bunch together to solve puzzles. After about five minutes of watching them play on their own, I know how much hosting I need to do. Specifically, I know how much hosting I'll need to do in order for them to have fun. If they haven't read the clues in front of them or even attempted to interact with the puzzle they'll need my guidance to keep enjoying the game. If they need me to just occasionally say, "yes that's right" or "Wow, you solved that really fast" then that's happily my job for the night.

If any group becomes overwhelmed by the puzzle experience, they will stop thinking about how to solve puzzles and will start to think instead about solving the problem of a bad night out. Do I comfort my idiot friend that suggested doing this now or later? To keep them from being overwhelmed focus on your game flow, both the flow you'll tailor to specific groups as well as the ones every group will experience. No matter what they group, they'll want calmer moments that are more story focused or help progress the story. Everyone wants to rally around points where they open the door to keep going or place down a very important object. A calm moment gives the players a chance to regroup their energy and get excited about the next round of puzzles. Calm moments can come from brief story scenes or hallways between main sections of the game. Treat your story scene like you treat your hallway: you never want either to last more than ten seconds. A quick ten second break is usually all a group needs to ramp up their energy again. If either drags on, the players will either resent the time stolen or worry that they're missing something. Why is the hallway so long if it is just a break between the main game segments?

A clear puzzle presentation also helps focus players. If they know they have all the equipment they need to solve a puzzle, then the moments spent solving it can be an exciting, focused time as they know they are nearing their next reward moment. When players are not sure if they should be working on a puzzle or instead searching for more context clues in the environment about how to solve it, vital energy will be lost. Players interacting with puzzles they aren't yet supposed to solve can introduce terrible red herrings as well. Players also tend to have a very immediate mindset. Missing pieces cannot be subtle, as the average player won't be thinking ahead but instead living in the moment. So if that moment requires them to become more and more creative to make sense of what they have then that is what they will do. I've made the mistake of adding ambiguous tools to my rooms several times and having players walk around unsure of what to do with the tool their carrying has always been a huge energy drop for me. The less the players need to return to puzzles, the better the gameplay flow.

Each puzzle has three essential energy moments when being engaged. The "cue," in which players know what to do and when they are supposed to do it. The "progression," in which they are doing the necessary tasks that are a part of the puzzle until they are completed. And the "feedback," in which they see what happens next. An intriguing cue, a fun progression, and a surprising feedback can each be energetic puzzle moments and rarely would you want to put all three together because one great moment usually subtracts from another. Let's go through some puzzles I've experienced that succeed and some puzzles I've made that failed on these individual points.

Most times a good cue for a puzzle is immediately knowing the why and when of a puzzle. When you come across a room full of lasers at various angles you immediately know you need to cross it without hitting the lasers. But if the players don't know when they're supposed to be doing something the cue can be the most excruciating experience in a room. For my Santa Claus themed room, I had them pick up a hacker box and plug it into a power station at the North Pole. My first problem was that the set design didn't make it immediately obvious it was a power station. The second is that the whole idea didn't make much contextual sense. Hackers at the North Pole? People would carry around their hacker box until we finally told them what to do next. Even then they wouldn't understand what they were doing, they would just do it. That's missing the cue entirely and just following instructions.

For a good progression puzzle, nothing can beat a fun arcade game. I had a game where we had to work as a team to roll three balls into a giant wooden machine, carefully shifting the wooden beams the balls rolled on into different positions. Working to move the beams was fun and the progression of the puzzle as we successfully placed ball after ball couldn't have been clearer. On the other hand, one of the puzzles I created myself had people manipulating a series of sliders to turn on the correct sequence of lights. No matter how many clues I give to the puzzle, it takes the majority of people far too long to understand how to make progress, and they'll push the sliders out of position over and over again.

Once completed, a good feedback from a puzzle is typically a door opening out of no where. The surprise as the entire landscape of the room changes is inescapable. When I was first working on electronic puzzles, though, I didn't understand how much they need sound and movement in their feedback. I had players enter in a color sequence that turned on a code they needed in a picture frame. Silently. I thought players would be confident enough in their answers to search the room after entering it in. Instead they would just press the correct sequence over and over until they finally gave up. Maybe someone would eventually see the sequence in the painting but more often than not we'd have to point it out to them.

Each puzzle moment should build the energy higher and higher. An especially fun IPE has players all but running to the next puzzle excited to start another round of cue, progression, and feedback. A slow game will have serious errors in all three.

The most important part of a game is the feedback it provides to players. Competitive head-to-head challenges in games have given a steady flow of feedback which is what makes them fun and challenging. Feedback also takes us back to hunting, as we trap creatures and force actions the excitement comes from knowing what the reaction will be so that we can master the pattern. The more immediate feedback the more the players can learn the processes that are the heart of the game and the better than can react to the challenges they are facing. Feedback is also another point of communication for a group to share as they can provide their own personalized commentary on what they are encountering.

Feedback is always positive for players and so should be offered to them as much as possible. Because feedback is a form of serving your guests, it becomes a reward in the room and people want to feel as rewarded as possible. The more immediate reactions a game can provide and respond to the more dynamic it feels. It should also never be subtle. Even the quiet opening of a game chest leaves an obviously open box that all the players can see. Feedback in of itself brings novelty to us and we love it both expected and unexpected in IPE environments.

Staff engagement gaining energy

People have standard expectations for their staff at entertainment events that have been in place for decades. Which is great for us! It gives us a framework that's easy to work with. Disney calls these expectations the four keys: safety, courtesy, show, and efficiency. Safety needs to be projected above all else, as people want to feel they are in a professional environment that will present to them only imaginary risks.

If people feel the equipment that they are playing with is truly unsafe, while they may still enjoy the game, they will not have the abundance of energy that comes from feeling safe to explore.

Courtesy makes players feel at ease and that their questions or concerns will be welcomed and readily answered. If people feel like they are not welcome in an environment, they will have a more difficult time relaxing and engaging it. This is especially true in environments where people are asked to engage in awkward moments they've never experienced before or moments in which they will certainly make mistake. A lack of courtesy keeps people on their guard and gives them a harder time expressing their ideas or interacting with each other. To be courteous to your players only requires two questions: "Hi! How has your day being going so far," and "Have you all played any Escape rooms before?" When all else fails, be sure to point out the bathroom. Your players will be ready to start solving puzzles in no time.

Show comes from the staff and the performances that make the players feel they are in a special environment. If the staff member takes the time to act dramatic and treat the world they are about to enter as real, the players will want to meet that energy and treat the world as real too. Acting invites play, and the more people are in the mood to play the better their energy will be when they do. However, be sure that players are always invited to play and not required to play in order to win. Players should always have the comfort level that most inspires them to engage the room. Modern theater famously terrifies audience members by assuming that everyone in the audience wants to share the spotlight and so will often force them into it. A quick speech given is always a good mood setter, but just remember any speeches or lengthy interactions with guests must be given before the clock begins ticking. I also personally recommend giving a speech in an environment without any clear puzzles present. I should never be more interesting than a puzzle in the room and I know I myself have played too many rooms where I can see a really interesting puzzle just past the game master.

When it comes to show, above all else, do not explain problems with the show. I once attended a room where, after giving a brief explanation that we were about to search for our, supposedly, murdered Uncle's will, she then went on to explain every puzzle we were about to experience in detail. In monotone, excruciating detail. By the time she had finished her five minute speech on how the locks didn't quite work in the room, what bulbs were burnt out and what puzzles they had removed from the room that we were never going to get to see (very useful information for obvious reasons) I was so tuned out that I missed her warning that we had to press "#" after entering the final door code in order to Escape. So, of course, smash cut to me entering the correct door code over and over in confusion because I was sure I had it right at the very end of the game. What if the surprise-killer Uncle was behind me, ready to stab me and reclaim his estate for himself? His last words to me would have been the very cinematic "You should have pressed #!" Lame show guys.

With that terrifying example of lack of showmanship behind us, let's go into a bit more depth with the ideas of show itself. A lot of theme parks use the code S.P.I.E.L. for their audience interactions: show, presentation, interaction, enthusiasm, and language.

Showing action is always better than describing it. When I'm telling the story of my game I show as many props as possible: portraits of the characters, demonstrations of parts of the show, and puzzles they'll be interacting with in the game.

Presentation gives the players a focal point for learning about the show. A clear speech point not only focuses the group but also gives them a chance to ask questions before the game begins. Rarely will a group have questions, but it is always good to be sure they are as settled as possible because you don't want someone distracted when it is time to solve puzzles.

Interaction is not just about interacting with the players in unique ways but also interacting with the environment like you are really responding to it. Instead of talking about the game, game hosts experience the game with the players by demonstrating certain items or "learning" facts about the environment for the first time. If the lights suddenly start to turn on and off, act like you've never seen that before. And if players expect unique traits from their host, then you alter your interactions with them to meet their standard as best you can.

Enthusiasm, in the context of an entertainment spiel, is totally fine to fake. It lends stakes to the game that might otherwise be missing. if the staff truly wants the world's problems to be solved and communicates that to the players that they must be the ones to solve it then they'll be more interested in the story. Telling the players that I truly believe they can solve the world's problems, even though I say "truly" to every group that passes almost always puts a smile on their faces. When the waiter says "great choice" you don't worry about whether or not they say that to all the guests, you believe that that your choice really was great.

And finally we come to language. Even though I have a particular speech written down, it's always a good idea to adjust the language if you know the group will respond more to an alteration. For example, if a group is more interested in scoring a great overall game time than listening to the story than I might bend the speech a bit to emphasize the clues in the speech more than the story. Or if someone's having a birthday, then perhaps that day is the key to their success in the room. A bit of special language really makes the group feel acknowledged and that they are uniquely in control of their situation.

So while there's a lot to remember and use in "showmanship," the final key, "efficiency," should never be overlooked. While somewhat more subtle than the other keys, efficiency is always appreciated because players want to feel the staff is making a good use of the time they bought for the experience. Efficiency basically boils down to the players sense that this is not the first time the staff has lead people through the experience professionally, and so things are certain to go well for them. An experienced staff member knows how to make the game fun for groups of every shape and size and it shows. A game host that is not overwhelmed by the experience, even if something clearly goes wrong during the show, keeps the audience engaged. For example, every once and a while the marble in the game does something it shouldn't. Instead of panicking and rushing off to consult the game master I retrieve a tool for just such an occasion (a stick) and hand it off to a player to give the marble a poke. While the game has gone wrong: it's gone wrong in a way I recognize and have prepared for. People don't mind if some of the extra ambitions of the show take a tumble sometimes; it's how they know they're part of live entertainment. What's more frustrating is when the crew of a game has arrogantly assumed everything will go right every time and hasn't built in any back-ups or resets into the game.

All of these keys control the reality of the game and a well-trained staff uses them to set a fun, energetic tone before the game even begins and keep it going long after the game ends. We usually go a step further and try to understand the group as much as possible before they arrive, judging them by their group size and if they have chosen to play on "easy" or "hard." We know one thing about every group: they have chosen to solve puzzles for fun, bond as a group, and challenge themselves. That actually already gives us a lot of information. Someone in that group has gone out the way to book the activity and should be actively encouraged that he or she has made the right call. Even if their friends do turn out to be less interested in the game, they will still feel the effort of arranging the night out was worth it. I've had plenty of grumpy Moms and Dads give a slight nod of approval on the way out the door. Getting an "Yeah, it was ok" from someone who doesn't get the experience is a lot better than the brutal, "We don't have to talk about it."

The Escape Game industry is an especially great place for the entertainment standard of the "5 minute" principle. That's finding the one moment needed to give each group a truly special time. For example, posing for a few extra pictures or giving them a mini backstage tour only takes an extra few minutes to accomplish but can be the special unique detail that makes your players into permanent advocates of your show. For one group, I led the kid most interested in our special effects into the computer room and let him press one of the panel buttons to activate a jump scare that surprised his sisters. He was able to run back to them with joy and say, "That one was me! I got ya'll!" There's a good chance he'll always remember that only took an extra minute of time.

Ways to give special moments include resetting a puzzle to let them play it again, telling a special story about the history of the game, giving IPE recommendations, or passing out special treats for the younger players. Because your staff will be spending at least an hour with each group there's ample opportunities to find exactly what they need to be true VIPs.

Media Apathy drains energy

Theme parks have increasingly had the issue of people not being interested in engaging in their experiences. The average person is there to experience as many fantastic moments as quickly as possible, but long lines always separate them from each exciting moment. So theme parks have introduced queue media to explain the story and that... has made the problem even worse. While people can appreciate entering the world of their favorite movie, they are not there to learn or listen to characters explain technology, just enjoy the environment. And that makes teaching about the plot and characters of the movies very difficult. The more complicated the plot the worse the media apathy becomes.

Similarly, people in puzzle rooms are there to explore and solve puzzles and so trying to tell complicated stories is always a distraction.

They want just enough of a story to convey a mood and help them understand the progression of the puzzles, not so much that they are expected to remember facts or experience complicated narrative twists in the story, like discovering that they were working for the villains all along. Because movies are chiefly about characters, a sudden betrayal can be an exciting plot point. But in an IPE, the environment itself must change if players have been "betrayed." Players want control of their actions, and they want to clearly understand the consequences of that control.

For example, one of the most common examples of a story twist is players "suddenly" discovering a vampire among them. In movies, this is turning around and seeing that one of your players has grown teeth and immediately attacking you. How do you convey this in an IPE environment? I had one game that had us break into witch's coven only to reveal that they were all secretly hiding Dracula's body to... kill him later, I guess. This was explained to us by a cat familiar as we waited... and waited and waited for a fireplace to move that was slowly being electronically lifted. We descended from a witch's cabin to a witch's basement that awkwardly had a coffin stuffed into one of the corners.

How could this have been better conveyed? Imagine if instead we were told to hide in a normal cabin because there is a vampire in the area. When we start to explore the cabin we discover a hidden room that hides the vampire's coffin. We have discovered the vampire's dwelling place and now we have less than an hour to kill him before he kills us!

How can you tell if your moment is introducing media apathy and draining the energy of a room? Imagine the dialogue set up for both situations if the scene is being narrated. "Look, the fireplace is opening! The witches have actually been hiding Dracula all along and now you have a chance to finish their work. If you descend into their basement you can find the right enchanted items to destroy him. Quickly now!" or "This must be Dracula's cabin! Quickly, now is your chance to kill him before he kills you!" And the real bonus of the second line of dialogue is that it's not really an explanation of the "twist" just a simple statement of the new facts dramatically delivered.

People want to make the moments and not watch them, so explaining is never going to be the best option. People want the greatest actions and discoveries to be a part of their adventure, so videos showing them approaching a mysterious mansion will never be as exciting as them approaching the mansion themselves.

Here's another example. You line people into a room. You show them a video explaining the set-up of a situation. They must find the true will of their father or they will lose their family estate. They have one hour before the will reading. They have traveled to the mansion and are now locked in the library by the sister. They will only have one hour to escape and find the will. Then the video stops playing and a door opens and they are in the mansion's library where they can finally begin to solve the problems of the world.

You have already solved multiple problems for them which would be intriguing to the players. How did they get to the mansion? How did they get inside of the mansion? What is the mansion itself like? We want our mansions to be the huge so how well can we judge the mansion just from being inside a room? And worse, why are we locked in the library? They will have to find the will to win, so why did the sister lock them in a room full of puzzles that eventually will lead to the will?

Now imagine the same set-up with a slightly different direction. You have your guests enter a horse carriage and shut the door. As they hear the carriage start moving the driver speaks to them through the roof. He tells them, because they are old friends, he will take them to the mansion. He knows their sister is a wicked person and hopes they are right that she must have hidden a will somewhere on the estate. But they have one hour before the will reading to discover the truth.

At that point the carriage door opens and they step out onto the magnificent mansion's personal graveyard. Finding their way to the estate requires opening the French doors that overlook the library. Luckily, the groundskeeper has hidden a key in his shack. You enter the library and now all you have to do is find the secret safe before time runs out!

The most important thing to keep in mind about these two scenarios is that they could cost the exact same to produce. You could have an incredibly beautiful library that players must slowly explore until they find the puzzles inside. Or you could have a carriage, graveyard, groundkeeper's shack, and library for the exact same budget. Players could sit inside carriage seats before the lights come on in the rest of the set. Some gravestones, a shed, and artificial turf are all easy buys. Replacing a door with a glass door is simple. And players enter the environment immediately knowing what to do and already knowing what their objects should be.

People know they are there to solve puzzles in a limited time frame, so setup's should take advantage of the puzzles: "How do we get into the mansion?" is a better puzzle then "What books are we looking for that are related to a cipher?" The story should be the questions that drive the puzzles and their solutions should drive all the spectacular moments of the show. When the players open the gravekeeper's shack, that should be when lighting flashes over the sky. As puzzles are the main language of the game, written and audio language needs to be minimized so they have even greater chances to shine. People more easily process pictures explanations and visual communication is also more universal, so players will not be as bogged down by misinterpretations when they are solving the game. The faster your players can process your game the better and the less the energy drains.

Hints and Objectives gaining energy

Failure must have a cost. Failure to complete a game either starts the puzzle over or clearly loses time. You can even open alternative puzzle paths that make the experience easier if players are particularly struggling with the main path. In my room we have a shortcut marble that the game master can drop if players are particularly struggling with the arcade portion of the game.

The hints and objectives that the staff gives players during the course of the game helps players come to the brink of failure but never actually fall into it. Giving hints and objectives during the course of a game are usually good energy boosts for the team. It can help them eliminate red herrings, confirm they are on the right path, or send them exploring again. I strongly encourage exploring with hints and objectives because the less of both typically the better the experience, but it is also good to have one active hint and one passive hint available on the site for each puzzle.

Objectives help players know what to do next and where to go. Ideally, players will need to be told as little about their objectives in the course of the game as each puzzle should immediately flow to the next clear obstacle. But devices and characters are sometimes needed to keep players focused, especially if there are limits in the environmental set-up that can cause players to lose valuable time. For example, providing objectives in a larger game environment is more essential then providing them in a small environment. Without that focus, players can start to give higher meaning to certain props or start inventing their own more complicated story ("maybe it's a test and we're supposed to tear the place apart!") Players imaginations and ingenuity can be their worst traits in a room because they can start imagining a path that is completely against the real one. Some of my smartest guests end up with the worst times.

Hints are different then objectives because they focus more on the "how" and the "what" than the "when and the "why" in puzzles. It is up to the game master and game host to decide when a group really needs a hint. Sometimes a group will be silently struggling but able to eventually come up with the answer. Sometimes they will simply be struggling and their energy will drop until it is gone. If the team is undoing the progress of their puzzles because of miscommunication then a well-delivered hint can unite them again.

Active hints are direct objectives, written instructions, and visual spotlights: each of which are clear components of the cue portion of a puzzle. Passive hints can be more easily over-looked media such as painting, letters, and sound cues. These types of clues will reward players that are deeply examining the environment. All of these hints are built into the environment and do not necessarily need to be pointed out by the staff. But they should be the hints that game masters and hosts point out before they start to improvise hints.

If properly managed, the passive hints are great for inexperienced teams or under-utilized players. The game host can call attention to the passive hints so that game-breaking hints do not need to be used to solve puzzles. And privately giving a hint to a player that is not engaged in a puzzle gives them the chance to feel more special and contribute to the group. Keeping the entire team engaged and busy throughout the experience means more energy and more fun.

Staff statements draining energy

A player should interact with a puzzle organically and never need instructions. That's the goal but we have hints and objectives helping us get there. However, even hints and objectives can fail us and then it will be up to the staff to provide the extra support necessary to solve the puzzle. The important factor here is that there should never be an extraneous explanation on the puzzle that removes players from the game. This could be just giving the answer, explaining a limitation of the technology, or providing step-by-step instructions of what to do. If players lose the chance of discovery and are instead simply being lead through the environment they are no longer playing in an "interactive puzzle exhibit" they are simply in a "puzzle exhibit." The game host becomes the docent leading from one puzzle to the next. And James Bond never stops to listen to the tour guide explain the enemy base. He sneaks off from the group to pursue action. A hero never encounters instructions on how to proceed during his quest, instead he figures out what he needs by responding to the environment and the challenges it presents. Anything else feels too "curated" to be fun.

During testing, a puzzle may be discovered to be not as easily engaging for players as the developers had hoped. The solution should never be "add more detailed instructions on how the controls work" but instead refining the meaning of the puzzle or even dropping it. Every good room should have some spare puzzle ideas to replace puzzles that aren't working out.

Out-of-game puzzle explanations always damage and cheapen the world being presented. Players want to feel that they are not just solving a puzzle that many groups have solved before but progressing through their experience. They want to be able to make-believe that they are turning on the factory's power, not just simply pressing a button. Breaking the imaginary world to give players outright instructions removes the reality you've been carefully building that they are heroes and turns the experience back into a managed team exercise.

Consider the difference between open ended questions and close ended questions. A close ended question is, "Do you like Sherlock Holmes?" or "What is your favorite Sherlock Holmes mystery?" The answer for the first is a "yes" or "no" and the answer for the second is reciting your favorite story. Open ended questions would be "Why do you like Sherlock Holmes?" and "What would be a mystery you would love to see Sherlock Holmes solve?" Each question now invites a personal response.

So in IPE's, instead of offering open-ended questions we provide open-ended statements. "The chest's second digit is written on the Captain's table" invites a "go" or "don't go" response: players either go to the table or they do not. "The captain would often write down the answers he needed" is an open-ended statements. It is up to players to infer that because the captain wrote answers down they should go to the table. Providing open-ended statements give you the chance to provide a lot more clues to the players but still have them solve the experience themselves. The more your staff is trained in providing good open-ended statements the more they can properly channel the energy of the game to each team.

Charting the game's entire energy

The energy throughout the game all channels into one final moment: winning the game. The boosts from exploring the environment must be actively managed by the game master and host through hints, otherwise the energy will be lost and the game will become work. The basic tenet of a game having successful energy is that the players should never feel like they are losing, even if they do not quite succeed in conquering the game. The challenges and progress of the game should be as clear as possible so that players actively know whether or not they are performing well in the game.

Let's review a few energy scenarios. The room itself in these scenarios will be considered objectively amazing. However, there will always be a group that needs help and that the staff will need to manage to ensure they have an excellent experience.

BAD ENERGY MODEL: CLEARLY LOSING TEAM

In the worst energy scenario, players actively know they are losing throughout the experience. The staff will introduce the players to the game and give them an amazing room to play. The problem begins when the staff starts giving open-ended statements that are not effective to the players. The staff does not direct them to the active or passive hints and then cannot provide statements that clue in the players on what to do next. Off this lack of communication players will stop asking for help and will run out of ideas on how to progress with the game. So the staff starts giving outright explanations to the puzzle that turns off the imagination of the players.

Even if players start to progress through the room they will have that clear "lose" on their record and will have a harder time immersing themselves in the experience. They may stop independently trying to engage the puzzles at all and will instead start to continuously ask the game master and host for hints. As this negative energy continues, players will get to the point when they realize that they are going to lose the game no matter what because they can visually see puzzles they have not yet even had a chance to engage. This will lead to a frustrating final five minutes when players won't even know if they should keep trying or just give up completely. If the final puzzles aren't especially fun or the story engaging, then the frustration is even higher.

Finally they lose the game. Because the story needs to be completed, the Game Host walks them through all the puzzles they did not get a chance to play, which can be especially disappointing if the final puzzles looked really fun (and they are, remember this is an amazing room). The game inevitably ends on a note of disappointment. The worst case scenario (and I've had this happen to me) is that the players leave apologizing for being "dumb." Assuring players that they're not "dumb" is a huge low. Players should only leave my rooms feeling that they are "too smart" and should have played on the hard setting.

And then there are just the people that aren't for IPEs. You've probably run into them when you've invited the wrong family or friends to play one of your rooms. These people just don't find puzzles engaging and will hate open-ended statements trying to engage them. It's rare among paying customers but it still happens.

"Perhaps you need to reflect on your situation" the game host will say, trying to prompt them to look at the mirror that has a number hidden in the corner.

"What?"

"Uh, often times, Rose would look into her vanity mirror and think about how to escape her life."

"Okay, but we're looking for a number."

"Perhaps your numbers feel cornered and you should mirror their situation."

"Garry, look in the corners of the room."

"No, I mean... If you stand in front of the mirror all should become clear."

"Okay, I'm in front of the mirror but nothing's happening."

"...Look at the corner of the mirror."

"The corner?"

"...There. In the right corner."

"Oh. Garry! Enter '425.'"

"...Where?"

"Where should he enter it?"

And so on. But I should note: if the team is clearly going to lose and clearly do not "get" escape rooms then there isn't much harm in removing the "interactive" from the "puzzle exhibit" and really acting like a docent. A team that doesn't want to engage the puzzles will appreciate leaving the room early and just being "shown" the puzzles. Trust me: they won't be asking how they compared to other teams or asking for other room recommendations. They'll leave satisfied knowing this "weird" experience is not for them.

GOOD ENERGY MODEL: BARELY LOSING TEAM

A good experience is one in which the players run out of time but the Game Host helps them through the final puzzle. This will be a group that bonds with the room but not quite on the level needed to win. They'll have a good amount of energy but struggle on certain puzzles that the game host can't easily prepare for. Typically they will not be able to understand the clues in the environment and will need more hands on control. However, they'll still enjoy the experience and usually will not mind when the game host works with them on the final puzzle.

NEUTRAL ENERGY MODEL: CLEARLY WINNING TEAM

A neutral experience is when players clearly win. This will typically be a larger group that are able to tackle all the puzzles at once and have excessive energy to do so. They won't need clues or open-ended statements from the staff and will have twenty minutes left on the clock (if you're lucky). If they asked for the easy experience and you couldn't persuade them to try a harder mode then they will probably still be satisfied with the experience. But if they beat everything quickly then your only chance is that the effects and storyline were engaging enough that they still appreciated the experience. You might also have the issue that too many of your puzzles are industry repeats that they have already seen. Even a deeply experienced team will struggle a bit when they are encountering a good puzzle they have never seen before. Bottom line is that they solved your room without ever interacting with the staff or really experiencing waves of energy in the room so they weren't engaged the way we like our teams to be.

GREAT ENERGY MODEL: BARELY WINNING TEAM

For a successfully run game, while there are still a few inevitable drops in energy, these drops will bounce into the successful finale for the players when they solve all the puzzles and makes for a deeply satisfying experience. The game will dip a bit as the players struggle, but in this scenario the active and passive hints are discovered by the players themselves so they help each other solve the puzzles. The staff almost never has to provide an open-ended statement and, if the do, it is a line that is deeply involved with the story. "Perhaps, if you knew were to listen, you could hear her sing one last time." The players learn the general flow of the world's puzzles and what is expected to solve them. They know they have enough time to "comfortably" win but not so much time

Eventually players may hit another wall in progress and will lose energy as they come to realize they require another official hint from the game master. But that final hint will be enough to have all the other puzzles "click" into place and they'll will get another boost from knowing that they have entered the game's finale and are clearly going to win. After winning and activating the finale, they can celebrate their success with the Game Host and get another boost of fun as they discuss the puzzles, take pictures, and enjoy being complimented on their hard earned success.

Common environment mistakes

We've discussed a lot of great elements to create amazing experiences in IPE rooms. However, there are certain elements that should be avoided, both in the environment and with the staff that damage the reality of the game.

Talk down to players

The most common mistake is to talk down to players in the environment, giving them rules against breaking or being rough with equipment that they would have assumed by common sense are already in place.

It is the temptation of every restaurant manager to put up a "No shirt, no shoes, no service!" sign. The idea is that it saves them from having an uncomfortable conversation when someone walks into a restaurant with a dripping wet swimsuit expecting to be served. With the sign you can show them that this is the standard policy of the restaurant and that you aren't specifically picking on them. But how often does the manager deal with clueless dripping wet customers? Every single customer will read the sign and their first impression will be that the management doesn't believe in establishing friendly relationships but only guarding property.

The first impression your customer has of your establishment is how you have prepared for their arrival. A friendly greeting from the staff and letting them know they are welcome to explore the environment makes them feel empowered. After all, if a rowdy group starts trying to break equipment, they will not be surprised if they are firmly told to stop. There is no need to prep good groups for bad experiences when bad groups will immediately understand why they are being reprimanded. Disney World has plans in place for rowdy guests, but they never share them with the good guests, making the guests feel safe and free to explore.

Players also typically don't try to break things until they're out of ideas. A lot of rooms have what one designer calls, "the breaking point." It's the point of the game when players become so frustrated at not knowing what to do next that they start ripping the room apart to see if that helps. Their first idea is never to tear apart the room: it is always the last resort. And you should make sure the game runs smoothly enough that they never want to get to that point.

Players can get over excited in the environment and pry things open, but that is an inherent risk of the gameplay experience. There should always be enough fun experiences that even if players do "accidentally" solve a puzzle or two they still get to enjoy the majority of the experience and not think that breaking puzzles is the right way to win the game.

One of the best ways to deal with rowdy customers is to have a "house lights" setting. When it's time to go, a bar will flip off the mood lighting and turn on the harsh house lights, acting as a clear signal that it's time to stop partying. If the players are getting too destructive, deliberately breaking the game's mood will have that same effect of snapping them out of their mindset. Turn on "normal" lights and have the Game Master warn them in a tone that is "breaking character" that if they keep being destructive the game will immediately end. That will make anyone pay attention. One company has the character wear headsets for these game breaking moments, to let the people know that this is not a part of the game but a clear break because something has gone wrong.

Stickers in games

When there are delicate items in a room, there is always a temptation to protect them with sticker message. Every player would get a clear message if the mirror in the haunted house had a sticker on its frame saying "THIS MIRROR IS NOT PART OF THE GAME! DO NOT REMOVE!" Who knew the slaves of the pharaoh and the fairies of the forest had access to staples.com? Warnings remind the players that they are not heroes but customers under careful observation.

The basic truth is this: There's no way to add stickers to a room and keep the environment "real." Sure, the Beast may be cranky in his enchanted castle and have a delicate rose tied directly to his heart, but even he didn't slap a sticker warning on the rose's glass cover.

Every person that steps through the door should be the hero that has come to save the world. Indiana Jones doesn't come across a sticker in the forbidden temple saying "Be considerate of the next tomb raider and remove the golden idol gently!"

Oftentimes the solution to stickers is to discourage the thought that the item should be moved. If a table should not be stood on, you can glue objects to it that would make it too difficult for the players to climb onto it. If the antique vase is delicate enough to necessitate a warning, put it out of reach on an upper platform or put it behind bars. Every fantasy environment has unique ways to display or protect items and you can use those ideas to expand your experience.

You can also see if making your environment easier to play might alleviate the player's distress. Players want to be having fun solving puzzles and not breaking items in frustration. And if all else fails, you can put warning signs into the environment as long as you do so "in character." The beast would never slap a sticker on his Rose case, but it would make sense for him to use his claws to scratch onto the glass the single word "FORBIDDEN!"

Almost all puzzle environments will have a character that could give instructions to the players, from a wizard to a serial killer. Writing warnings as characters can be a fun expression of the element of language in your room. If you're worried that using warning language will tempt players to mess with your item, then your puzzle development has moved in the wrong direction. The more a player is tempted to mess with something the more they should be able to, and, indeed the more the room should expect them to. Rooms should give you the freedom to jump on the couch, not politely sit on it. But a warning not to touch delicate equipment, which clearly is delicate and not something the players would be tempted to handle unless they felt they had to, helps players appreciate the richness of the world they have been given complete control over. Players don't mind seeing display cases as long as opening the display wouldn't be more fun.

You can also put stronger warnings in out-of-sight places that the players should never realistically be seeing. If the players move a mat that they're not supposed to with a "take everything apart" strategy to solving a room, then you can have a game breaking warning sign that they are clearly straying outside of the boundaries of their game. The bottom of the couch can have a "Please do not move the couch" warning. The top of the couch shouldn't.

In my rooms, when something needs to be inaccessible to players but still accessible to management between games, I use fob keys, magnetic latches, and fake panels. Because the players never see a key hole or lock they never think that they'll need to interact with the object, even if it's a door that could clearly open otherwise. So if they see that Rose and it says "Forbidden!" on it and it is magnetically sealed with only employees being able to disengage the lock, any player that pulls at the glass case once or twice will learn that it is really a forbidden object and move on to another element in the room.

Also, if reset panels are in out of the way places that require players to crouch or stand on ladders, they're less likely to engage the prop in inappropriate ways. They're not going to get a ladder to enact with the environment so reset elements on high ledges are safe.

Face-planting into the painted tunnel

Every door that looks inviting should be explored. Rooms are the chance for players to fulfill their childhood dream of roaming forbidden environments and discovering the secrets hidden in the nooks and crannies. Places we can't go as children because they're private, dangerous, or hold terrible secrets are exactly why we want to explore them as adults.

While it's great to give players the sense that they're in a true place with more rooms then they need to visit they should never be disappointed by limitations. If you're on a train, you want to see all the compartments. If you're in a hotel, you want to see multiple rooms. That's because you never get to experience multiple cars of a train or hotel rooms in real life. It's exciting to confirm that you're in a place truly built for multiple people. However, you wouldn't want to naturally visit multiple floors of a hotel, so there are natural limits to our desire to explore environments. That means you can eventually block additional access without hurting the curiosity of the player. Players may want to explore one room of a flower shop but they wouldn't be interested in exploring multiple rooms.

A "forbidden" place usually means it is a place only for those with special training or privileges, and so it has been prepared for unique experiences. If the player is in a restaurant and they don't get to see the kitchen, they'll be disappointed because the kitchen is the special part of the restaurant they don't normally see. They don't need to see the bathroom, because they've been in plenty of restaurant bathrooms. It's exciting to feel like you're gaining privilege and prestige by solving puzzles and unlocking secret places.

Another danger is displaying "cool" props that you haven't prepared for the players to touch. Everything in the environment is a toy. Nothing is off limits. Because players bring their own kinetics to the environment, they're allowed to revert back to the child that leaves a play room in ruins because they know the parent will pick up after them. Making a mess is always fun. Not being able to play in your parent's dining room because that's where the "good china" is just makes you really, really want to play with the china. Even if you'd have no idea what to do with it, just the idea that you can't touch it makes touching it all the cooler. A good rule of thumb for development is that all props in the game are accessible by players and are cheap and easy to replace.

Expensive props can still exist but they should be in clear separate display areas. And better yet props can seem really expensive but actually be very cheap. Like dining china plates that are really plastic. Then the players finally get the chance to touch the china and live the dream.

Removing player smart phones

I know that is controversial take because a lot of owners don't want to have players take pictures of their room, but I think it is important to understand just how much we are cutting into the puzzle solving capacity of our players by removing their smart phones in a room. Removing smart phones really goes against a lot of the core energy we try to give to players.

One of the main components of an IPE game is that we are able to use the resources we already enjoy and have learned to use in a unique environment. If we were actually in a difficult situation the first thing we would probably do is use our phones to try and find a way out of it. Smart phones are the Swiss Army tool of the modern age and it is an essence of fun to be in situations in which we need to use them.

When we have a good thing going we like to keep doing it. Removing the smart phone and having people struggle with puzzles without it is removing the most essential tool people have trained themselves to use.

And people enjoy seeing media of an experience. To enjoy every moment of an IPE game would require watching about 60 minutes of footage and it would not truly capture the experience. An IPE game is not a passive movie experience but a full interactive adventure that is automatically personalized by the people playing it. There is no reason to fear players sharing the media of the experience because it just enhances their enjoyment of it and gives them another chance to be the true hero of the environment. A hero usually brags about how heroic they are so give your players the chance to do the same.

Some people also want the ability to leave the game in case of certain emergencies. Truly having a free hour is a luxury to parents, for example, who might be contacted for a variety of emergencies or semi-emergencies. It's not up to us to dictate just how dedicated someone needs to be to an experience so we frustrate more casual players every time we insist on putting the phone in the box. It's still of course up to every room to decide on their own these policies but removing phones will almost always lower the energy and fun in a room and not raise it.

Stiff corporate environment

The worst game environments I've encountered all feel like an office park. No matter how rich the gameplay, the choice of a corporate feel gives the rooms a bland, neutral touch where "one size fits all." Corporate places are deliberately designed to be as non-threatening as possible, which means they will never have a strong personality. Yet, when we go to theme parks we love to step into environment after environment of unique and interesting expressions. Stiff chairs, walls of photos, and various unrelated games give the feeling that you are in a doctor's office. If people don't feel special in your lobby than they will likely not feel special in your room.

However, much worse is when the room itself feels corporate. A corporate environment builds off an essence of interchangeability. A cubicle can be filled by anyone in an instant, with the only mark of personality allowed an easily replaced picture or toy. The entire staff can rotate week to week and no operations will change. This does not invite the idea that the players are special or will become heroes. Your room needs to feel like it is literally changing by the hands of the players. If your room feels like the game reset is a simple shuffling of papers and locks, players won't have fond memories of the environment. The more fun the environment, the more challenging the reset. A great reset is part of a room's planning process, so that a lot can be accomplished in a little time. But a complicated reset should never limit the awesome ideas you want to give to your players. If the choice is between having an easy "corporate" reset and a challenging individualistic one, always choose the individual.

Use dynamite to explode the cave and figure out how you'll pick up the rocks between games later. Often, you'll eventually come up with just as many cool ideas and tricks that will go into the reset challenges as much as the rest of the room's challenges. For example, in one of my rooms we had larger-than-life blocks that had to be inserted into a wall. The players enjoyed moving the blocks as a team, but the game master had to reset the blocks alone and it was a real pain. Eventually I had the idea to buy a dolly tool and put it in the room. Now moving the blocks isn't nearly as frustrating.

PUTTING TOGETHER YOUR PUZZLES

Puzzles are what it's truly all about. If you skipped over the previous chapters of this book to start reading here, then you're probably my favorite, don't tell the people reading the other chapters. Choosing the best possible puzzle for a room, requires a lot of thought, research, and planning. Then you have to do it again and again until you have about a hundred appropriate puzzles for the room. Once that you can start factoring in the puzzle type, player participation parameter, puzzle value, puzzle controls, and the in-world puzzle profile: everything factors in to breathing life into your world. And after everything you've got to check the reset sequence!

Bottom line, the more time and energy spent creating the most spectacular puzzles for the environment, the more your players will love the experience, even if a puzzle or two proves too challenging for the team. The silver lining in all this work? The best puzzle is not necessarily the most expensive puzzle. It's the most memorable. Some of the puzzles that I've enjoyed solving the most were incredibly simple, just a box and some objects. If you're on track for the next great (but super cheap) IPE, do it!

Puzzle Controls

Every puzzle has two essential components: the lock and the key. These components can be completely separate or seamlessly linked together. They can be wood, metal, or electronic. They can be in the form of combinations, buttons, or electronic touchpads.

In a room the first thing people scan for is the puzzle controls so that they know what they will be expected to solve. Puzzle interfaces are always important gathering points for players, so it is important to present as much variation between them as possible. So let's try and break down some of the most commonly used locks and keys.

Locks

Locks have one function: to be where the keys will be used. They either accept specific information or specific objects to be unlocked. They will sometimes give clues to the cue and progression of a puzzle, but they will always be the central point of feedback. Many locks are used in boxes that hold additional puzzles and puzzle components, but locks can open doors, turn on lights, activate sounds, begin animations, and change just about anything in the players' world.

Dials

Dials are used in combination locks. Setting them all to the correct number will unlock the device. The correct formation for the lock is usually found in a secondary puzzle, such as a code written down somewhere in the room. There are many 3-5 dial locks on the market, but higher than five must be custom-made.

Buttons

9 Button grid

Used for classic doorway entry codes and fits the basic alphanumeric pad people are used to seeing on their phones. They can be good for word codes that are longer than four or five letters.

6 Button panel

A custom-made panel often used for color puzzles. Great either in one row of six or two rows of three. A common color combination used for puzzles is: Blue, black, gray, pink (red), white, green. Another good combination is: Red, orange, yellow, green, blue, violet.

4 button panel

Four button panels (such as the master directional lock) are great for compass and avatar movements on a map. They can translate to "Up," "down," "left," and "right" or "North," "South," "East," "West" but have been used for many visual sequences in rooms.

Sensors

1-to-1 Fob

Electronic locks often used to open doorways or compartments. Fobs can often be hidden in objects to make gameplay more organic to players.

RFID tags

Sensors often used to create object placement puzzles. RFID tags are used for more complicated electronic sequencing puzzles.

Motion Detectors

Basic motion sensors are good for puzzles that require physical expression, like dancing, ducking, or shooting.

On-off switches

On-and off switches are good for simple choice puzzles. On and off interfaces are great for a variety of puzzles because binary feedback can easily fit into all puzzle types.

Magnets

Most often used for electronic controls that, when solved, turn off the electricity to the magnet and automatically open the compartment but can also be good for hiding latches that are unlocked by the players using various tools.

Capacitive (touchscreen)

Capacitive touchscreen technology works great with smart tablet interfaces. Can be used to program unique gameplay sequences.

Stepping pads

Stepping pads are great for puzzles that require more direct physical expression from the players and when steps are being emphasized in a puzzle.

Keys

Keys can be everything from physical keys to the information required to open a lock. They can be found, made, or even performed by players.

Skeleton keys

Skeleton keys are long, solid, and one shape. The lock key hole are usually larger to fit these types of keys.

Cabinet Key

Cabinet keys are short and have a unique lock shape that can easily be identified by its more round shape.

Electric Key

Electric keys use computer controls in conjunction with magnet locks or retractable latches that activate when the key is near the sensor.

Magnets

The use of magnets can uncover hidden answers, such as dropping magnetic dice and having them face one direction to display the correct code or only have an arrow point in one specific direction to reveal a specific word.

Screens

A screen can display the answer to a puzzle when the puzzle is solved. This can be the use of tv screens, smart tablets, or projectors. It should be noted that players often time need sound cues to accompany screen changes.

Objects

Any object can be a key simply by having an answer written on it. But the more organic use of objects in a room the more players enjoy a special experience because, while they can run across standard keys in their everyday life, they will never use objects as locks.

Paper

Paper is used to convey riddles, clues, and mathematical problems. It should always be very theme specific when used in rooms because it is too easy for players to play paper puzzles in more everyday circumstances, such as puzzle games at home. It can also be frustrating to players when they are not allowed to write answers on the paper itself as a lot of paper puzzles have trial and error elements to them.

Blocks

Blocks can be placed in a specific pattern to reveal a code on one of their sides. They can also be stacked in ways that eliminate incorrect options or reveal a larger pattern solution.

Planks

Planks can be placed to reveal a code or message when shifted into certain positions.

Light

Lights are one of the most fun key elements for players because there are so many ways to use them but also because they require set-up unique to the IPE industry.

Shadows

Shadows can reveal the shapes of numbers and letters by shining lights on specific objects or from hidden sources.

Colors

Colors can be turned on and off with lights or onto objects to reveal a color code answer.

Spotlights

Direct and indirect light sources can be used to highlight secret compartments that need to be investigated by the player or have become important as the story progresses.

Puzzle Types

I've analyzed, well, at least a thousand puzzles so far if not more, and I think they can be pretty readily condensed into ten general puzzle types. A well-balanced room should highlight each type at least once to provide players a truly balanced experience. While many type components can overlap in a puzzle, there will ultimately be a chief type that stands out. For example, a puzzle that requires players to feel multiple items and then add them together into a mathematical formula code could be considered either a sensory puzzle or a code puzzle. If the players spend more time writing out and solving the code than they do feeling the individual pieces, then it ultimately would classify better as a code puzzle. If, however, all they need to do is figure out what they are feeling in order to match shapes to a corresponding number code then the puzzle is sensory.

Another example would be a maze that requires a tool to use it. If the maze is simple and the tool is difficult to use (such as a maze on the ceiling with a key inside that must be fetched using a pole with a magnet on top) then the puzzle should be classified as a tool puzzle. But if the magnet tool is easy to use and players spend more time charting out the correct path out of an intricate maze, then it is a maze type puzzle.

A room that uses all the types of puzzles at least once is dynamic and better engages players and satisfies everyone's desire for novelty and surprise. After solving four riddles in a row, even if they are varied and well-constructed, then needing to solve another riddle can start to drag down the energy of the room. Entering a room with a ton of 3-digit combination locks always worries my team and the room had better be really amazing to make up for it.

Before analyzing the types in more depth, it will be useful to analyze the four basic components that make up a puzzle. These components will be the requirements to solve a puzzle and each puzzle type highlights different components.

Thought

A puzzle high in "thought" requirements can be processed independently without players even needing to physically interact with the puzzle interface, such as studying a maze to determine the best possible path on it or thinking through a riddle. If you can be confident you know the answer simply by looking at the puzzle, it is a high thought puzzle.

Skill

Skill is the exact opposite, with requiring hands-on control and practice in order to solve the puzzle. Skills should always be easy to learn in the room and not require any true athletic skill, but players with athletic skills should definitely have a bit of a bonus in solving these puzzles. Using your senses particularly well or having good hand-eye coordination should always make these puzzles easier. Puzzles that reward interaction are high skill puzzles.

Luck

Like when gambling, luck is an exciting factor for players to interact with in games. If they get lucky solving a puzzle, they feel that they have earned something special and unique to their experience. While you never want to have a puzzle have such high level of chance that unlucky players would lose more than a minute or two of time on a bad run, having a chance component brings an exciting dimension to the overall "ticking clock" challenge that IPE games always have. However, it should always be clear that chance is involved so that players do not think they need to find missing components before they will be able to solve the puzzle. If you have a puzzle element that changes every time and cannot be altered by skill or thought then you have a high luck puzzle.

Time

Some puzzles have a main component of time. While the goal is clear to the players, it takes time to get there. A jigsaw puzzle has a fairly obvious goal but still takes time to assemble all the pieces and complete the puzzle. This helps engage players that may not want to deal with skill or thought challenges in the room while also increasing the excitement of having to work against the clock. If you have a puzzle that could easily be accomplished by one person (even with their hand tied behind their back) as long as they had enough time to focus on it, you have a high time puzzle.

Arcade puzzles: Skill and luck

These are the games everyone loves to play at carnivals and would win with enough patience, skill, time, and dollars. But these arcade games are better than the midway because they can be adjusted to ensure quicker success and that less skill is required to master them. You can also teach tricks to players that reveal "shortcuts" to playing because in puzzle rooms you get to play these games until you win and you get to play them unsupervised. Throw the ball, launch the arrow, or trace the metal wire through the loop: you get the unlimited resets you need to master the puzzle and be the carnival hero.

All arcade puzzles are a combination of skill and luck. There is a simple objective to follow through to completion. These puzzles are great for hero moments as a less engaged player can practice the skill for a few minutes and score a huge win for the rest of the team. They are also great for innovative team moments when other players have a chance to assist each other and make the arcade challenge easier by having supportive roles.

Arcade moments typically work well as movie moments in the game's story because they are easy to make larger than life. If you can win the arcade puzzle the first time through you feel like a real champion defying the odds and saving the day. They're especially fun at the beginning of the game when players feel they have tons of time to accomplish the goals they need. For every active arcade game puzzle it is a good idea to have at least one other puzzle active that engages thought or time components for the other players to focus upon.

A unique fun aspect of arcade puzzles is that there are usually ways to cheat at them if the players think through the mechanics enough. Can they stand on a chair and bypass using a pole to instead just use a magnet to navigate a maze on the ceiling? Can they put their fingers in between a wire game to ensure the two pieces of metal never touch? A good game rewards outside-the-box thinking. Arcade games are a good reward for the competitive thinkers in the group looking for especially clever ways to solve the challenges. They don't simply want to compete against the room but against the room's designer as well. Arcade games need to be more durable both for excited and frustrated players who will be harder with the equipment than other props inside the room.

Players are allowed to have fun by cheating, but cheating should lose the rewards of special effects or cool moments. Players shouldn't want to cheat because they don't want to miss out on every special game moment. They call it emergent behavior: Everything the designer did not see the player doing that emerges from the general gameplay: loopholes and exploits. Good storytelling will bring balance to this temptation people won't be tempted to cheat if it means skipping cool parts of the story.

Arcade puzzles are best when all the pieces needed for the puzzle are clearly grouped together so they understand the process required to win. It can be frustrating to watch one player attempt an arcade puzzle and not be able to at least assist in some way (such as blocking holes at certain times) so it is good to design puzzles that give other players the chance to be helpers and lower the amount of skill required. For instance, the air gun they're using to shoot has more power if another player charges it while the main player is firing.

Example of poor design:

One game I played took place in a country club setting. At one point we had to set up obstacles in the correct pattern and then putt a golf ball through the course. However, setting up the obstacles was the actual solution to the puzzle and putting the ball itself was an afterthought. To complete the puzzle you could just drop the ball into the golf cup. What made the puzzle more frustrating was that if the ball was dropped into the cup and the obstacles were not in the correct place than you could not reset the game yourself and the staff had to manually come into the room to reset the puzzle for you by giving you more golf balls. This could have easily been solved by simply adding a track that rolls the ball back to a retrievable position for the players but they hadn't designed that element for the players.

This puzzle had several problems. The first was that it was not truly an arcade puzzle at all, as solving it did not require any physical action, just moving the pieces around. And since the game could not be reset there was no chance of improving the skill required for the game and, in fact, if you were lucky enough to hit a hole in one you could hurt your chances at solving the puzzle. The company had put up a sign warning people not to play putt-putt... on a putt-putt course. Not rewarding skill and luck makes for a bad arcade game experience.

Example of good design:

In a mad scientist room we had an oversized slot machine with flippers we had to control ourselves to guide the balls into the correct positions. The team had to work together to adjust the flippers before rolling the balls and communication was essential to get all the pieces into the correct places. It was the perfect puzzle for the start of the game because it got everyone talking and ready to work together to solve more puzzles.

Assembly puzzles: time and thought

Assembly puzzles have the basic gameplay structure of jigsaw puzzles and are all about organization and the correct placement of pieces. These puzzles are not the best for team moments because players can become distracted by arguing about how to proceed or even reverse progress made by other players, but are good for more quiet team members that want easier mental challenges in the room.

A combination of time and thought, these are jigsaw puzzles, construction puzzles, or puzzles with a clear progression of steps. They are perfect for players that like clear marks of progress when playing. Assembly puzzles always take an amount of time to accomplish and lends themselves to various branches of thought as players experiment with the best way to progress. Just as people solve a jigsaw puzzle in various ways (like searching for the corner pieces first), assembly puzzles can lend themselves to various ways of sorting and trial by error. Players don't necessarily need to start with all the pieces that will be assembled to begin solving the puzzle, but should be clear to the players that pieces are missing before they begin experimenting. For example, if the pieces are given in batches then it should be clear when batches are still missing, like having pieces that should clearly connect (say two halves of a face) separate from each other.

Example of poor design:

In a medieval themed room I played, we had to set up a group of irregular shapes into one uniform, specific cube pattern. When the correct cube pattern was assembled, one of the colored sides of the cube would reveal the number answer to a code. However, it was not clear that the sides needed to be assembled by color for the code to be revealed, and the amount of the time to solve the puzzle was about twenty minutes for my teammate, much too long to be working on any one puzzle in a room. As a general rule, no single puzzle should take more than 10 minutes for any group to play. Worse, because the amount of time spent on the puzzle was so long and the progression of the puzzle was not clear, I kept returning to the puzzle trying to help and could not focus on the other parts of the game. An assembly puzzle is the most fun when people have a clear goal of what they are assembling.

Example of good design:

In a spy room we had to find ten "bugs" hidden in the room and collect them all on a tray. We had to look through clothing, on top of desks, and behind posters to find them all. The best way to search the room was to work together and compare methods so we knew the most efficient way to search next.

Code puzzles: time and thought

Code puzzles are the translation based puzzles that have us match symbols, numbers, and letters to learn obscured answers. It can involve devices, equations, and even groups of objects. Code puzzles typically shouldn't be so complicated to over whelm the players but are a well used staple of puzzle design and should be incorporated whenever logical for the story's progression.

Players will usually spend half of the puzzle learning the requirements for translating the puzzle and the other half actually deciphering the correct sequence. The time portion that code puzzles required can be especially intriguing because players can see the code come alive in front of the them and guess at what the completed state might be.

Example of bad design:

The very last puzzle in a room was a code translation puzzle that required a tedious letter by letter cipher of instructions to solve. I tried to translate the necessary statements on how to win but we ran out of time. The translation could not have been tackled by multiple people at once because of the cipher tool that needed to be used and, as this was a late stage of the game, everyone else had to awkwardly wait for me to finish. The tension of my failure to translate fast enough for my team left an especially bad aftertaste upon losing the room.

Example of good design:

In a serial killer room there was a chain on a wall surrounded by a circle of letters. During the game we uncovered bios of the victims, each killed at a different time. Using the times of their death, we moved the chain to the correct "time" on the circle and were able to uncover a hidden word. It was an incredibly clever use of basic forensic information displayed in a way that naturally looked creepy and "in character" for a serial killer's basement.

Experiment puzzles: time and luck

Experiment puzzles have us guess until we find the one particular combination that fits the situation. With thought and skill minimized, time and luck become the stars of experiment puzzles. Given that time and luck together are components the players cannot control, experiment puzzles are usually the least fun to play in a room and so must be the most carefully managed of all puzzle types.

It can be hard to make it clear enough to players that you're expecting them to fidget with something until they figure out how it works.

Once people stop interacting with a particular puzzle it can be hard to get them to return focus to it. You have to make the communication and goal very clear and it's usually best if the experimentation is focused on a specific item, such as figuring out an electronic interface or which rope to pull to release an item. Experimentation is most fun when you have a hypothesis and you're testing out different responses. So players should know what result they're trying to achieve.

These are usually the math and word puzzles presented in a room. We are able to enjoy experimenting with math and vocabulary because we've already experienced the dynamics of these puzzles independently of playing a IPE game. When we see a riddle, we recognize the structure and know that we are supposed to make guesses. However, because riddles will rely on outside knowledge, players that are not able to solve the puzzle will bring the room to a dead halt.

Example of bad design:

In a time machine game, we were presented with a large assortment of switches that made the time displayed on the wall go up and down. There was no way to confirm how the grouping of the switches worked or even the exact amount the switches were making the clock go up and down. Rather, you had to generally guess by switching each individual toggle back and forth and deciding if it was getting you closer or farther away from the number you needed. Worse, the final number was unclear as it had to be derived from a previous code puzzle. Since there was no concrete certainty that you were closing in on the correct number, experimenting became frustrating.

Example of good design:

In a witch's cabin, we had various ingredients labeled in jars and a recipe for a potion. The only problem was that half of the recipe was torn out of the book. Experimenting with the jars and a weight balancer we were able to find the correct portions we needed for the spell. We had just enough variables in the puzzle that experimenting with the jars was fun and engaging.

Game puzzles: skill and thought

Game puzzles have specific rules we need to follow to win, and they are often like board games. These puzzles can be everything from matching games to elimination games. Almost all games are competition based or have automatic responses. Games always have rules and restrictions on movements and choices. The easier it is for players to learn the rules of a game, the better.

While most games are thought based, many have levels of skill required, from being able to take advantage of a sudden opportunity (such as an opening in a card game that only the fastest player can receive) to guiding vehicles and avatars.

The key to a game is that it will always have a core mechanic. Other puzzles may or may not have core dynamics but a game always must. The moving pieces and mechanics could be about helping players with various strategies: estimate, optimize, match, balance, classify, fetch, focus. The core mechanics help us either eliminate or order the pieces.

Usually a game in of itself with keep their core mechanics more hidden. Checkers has a hidden core mechanic of optimization. Classic games consist of relatively few systems that fit together elegantly. The more clear and refined the system the more a player will love the game. The more the variations on the system that organically evolve from the core mechanic the better. When introducing a game puzzle it is important that the core dynamic is revealed as clearly as possible to the players.

Example of poor design:

In one room we had to solve a game by figuring out the minimal amount of moves it would take to solve the "frog jumping puzzle" that requires switching all pieces to the opposite side using limited movements. We had to set up and play the game ourselves and, worse, there was no clear understanding of when we had finished, as once we thought we had the answer we had to call the answer to the Game Master through a walkie talkie and see if we were correct. The game became one of the most tedious parts of the room as we set up the frogs over and over to see if this time we had the optimal amount of jumps.

Example of good design:

In a room I designed, we created a miniature version of the "lights out" game. Instead of a 5 by 5 grid we only had a 4 by 4 grid that greatly simplified gameplay. We used the outside row to have a lights permanently "on" which helped cue the player that the progression of the game was the rest of the lights. We also used a lighter prop to "turn" on the lights by tapping each light with the lighter to turn "on" the light which players quickly understood how to use.

Lateral thinking puzzles: thought and luck

Lateral puzzles require unique or sudden shifts in thinking. Players will use objects used in strange ways such as blacklight flashlights shined on walls to find secret messages. Lateral thinking depends on leaps in logic that players will eventually make. This requires a bit of luck as they must be in just the right mindset to make the correct observation. However, unlike experimentation puzzles, players are in more control as they only need to make one logical leap before they understand the puzzle as thinking through the solution is more possible and can even be immediately done.

One of the greatest problems of lateral thinking puzzles is that people can get very misdirected. Not understanding how they are supposed to work or what they are supposed to represent can cause players to get "locked" into elaborate theories on how they are supposed to work which will require the game master to correct through hints. Another issue is that lateral puzzles can be "high risk/high reward" in making players look especially smart or foolish. A player that is able to immediately "see through" a lateral puzzle will be highly applauded by the group, but a player that stubbornly insists on his or her theory for a puzzle can drag a group down more than in any other puzzle category.

Example of poor design:

In the Country Club game, we had to shine a black light on the wall to find hidden markings. Not only was a black light puzzle weird for a country club setting, but it was easy to overlook the markings on the large wall mural they were hidden in so we spent a lot of time randomly looking for the answer. If the lateral puzzle has a large game area it will be difficult for them to have the "a-ha!" moment that will deliver the right solution.

Example of good design:

In an Edgar Allen Poe game, we retrieved a golden heart medal from a treasure chest. In a coffin was a soldier with a hole in his chest. It was clear that we had to put the medal onto his chest but not clear why. When we did, he sprung backward and revealed an entirely different room. Recognizing that we somehow needed to "complete" the solider brought us incredibly surprising feedback.

Maze puzzles: time and thought

Maze puzzles are one of the easiest visual markers in IPE games as we easily recognize their composition of twisting turns and dead ends. Mazes can have one path or multiple paths, but most often with a bird's eye view of the entire field. Mazes can be fun challenge to conquer, but also can be frustrating if the team has to watch one player have a hero moment because of the time component every maze requires by only having one guiding piece inside of it. It is best to always have another active puzzle to pursue while mazes are being run.

Given their general structure, mazes can be some of the most fluid designs in IPE games as the choices in direction can built in all shapes and sizes, from poking through a series of overlapping holes to driving vehicles through mystery corridors. A wide variety of tools can also be incorporated into maze games and add various skill components to their execution.

However, given the freedom of form in mazes, game specific context requires a greater focus in their creation. Mazes would slow down the world's characters, so it should be clear why they are there, One could use mazes as more of a metaphor for complexity in games. Instead of working a complicated machine, guiding a marble through it provides the idea that you are using the machine itself. Or instead of working through multiple levels of a temple, the maze can represent how large the temple truly is.

Example of poor design:

One room had a really amazing haunted house design. You were in a hotel and had to retrieve 13 keys that were hidden in puzzles throughout the room. This key was in plain sight, however, inside of a wooden maze stuck against a wall. By moving a block attached to the maze you would soon be able to retrieve the block and the key. But the maze made no sense in the context of the haunted hotel and was a straightforward labyrinth. Having a room key trapped in a maze would slow down the ghostly staff. With nothing special about the maze, the fact that it did not fit into the story of such an incredibly designed room became especially distracting. Mazes are a great addition to rooms, but they should always be able to fit into the larger context of the story and environment.

Example of good design:

In a prison game, we were locked in different cells. Removing the panel from my cell I could see the key to my cell inside of a maze. The player on the other side had to guide a magnet through the maze by following my directions. Once it got close to a hole at the bottom of the maze I could finally retrieve the magnet. The maze was made even more exciting by having to use the magnet to move the key "up" against gravity in certain parts of the maze.

Sensory puzzles: skill and luck

These puzzles use sight, taste, sound, balance, smell, and feel. They are great for people that might struggle with other puzzles challenges and can require more communication than other puzzles.

These puzzles are chiefly built around the skill of using the senses, but there is also definite luck components to them as people need to be able to trust their senses and memory well enough to understand what they are processing. The better the memory of a "pine" scent, the more players can be sure they have identified it correctly in the room.

Sensory puzzles can be uniquely fun for some players. They very memorable puzzles in games. They usually take extra time to maintain but are worth it for the more dynamic experience they create. If the environment and story easily support the addition of a sensory puzzle then they are well worth designing into a room.

Example of poor design:

One of the unique challenges of sensory puzzles is that they can be the most easy for players to break. I once played a room that was supposed to have a "feel" puzzle, but the cloth was broken so you could actually see the letters that you were supposed to only be able to touch. Not understanding that the puzzle was broken, it was especially confusing to see the solution in front of us.

Another time I created a smell puzzle for a Santa room but didn't give my players a chance to reset their sense of smell with neutral smells. I also tried to exclusively use sweet smells so the players had a difficult time differentiating between them. What should have been one of the more fun puzzles in the room ended up slowing down the teams and grinding the climax to a halt.

Example of good design:

In a Japanese room we had to prove ourselves worthy of the way of the samurai. One of our tests was to find the five scents mentioned in a haiku: pine, lemon, rose, grass, and leather. We had distinct bottles to use to find these scents and put them into the correct order. It felt like we were preparing a Japanese tea ceremony and was by far the coolest moment in the room.

Tool puzzles: skill and thought

Tool puzzles are anything that require objects to solve. One of the greatest joys is learning how to use a new tool, from the movies of James Bond to the games of Legend of Zelda. Tools are stock and trade for most hero stories. The tool is the intellectual's weapon, and it is able to engineer traps as well as engage shortcuts.

Every tool puzzle requires a degree of thinking, from understanding the need of the environment to understanding how the tool works. Most tools, however, require skill to manipulate and use the tool in the environment. Fishing tools, for example, can take a few tries before they are able to hook an item from the bottom of a fish tank.

One of the greatest temptations of a game designer is to create completely unique tools or use tools in decidedly strange ways in rooms. This should be dealt with cautiously, because adding confusing elements to the use of tools can make them too difficult. It can also be challenging to explain strange tools in the room's story and their use in a room can be a jarring out-of-context experience. A noticeably electronic tool in a pirate setting is difficult to ignore.

Example of poor puzzle design:

For the Santa room, I thought it would be cool if players had a hacker box that they needed to plug into a console to override the system and turn the power back on in Santa's factory. However, it did not occur to me how difficult it would be for people to understand they needed to use a sci-fi "high tech tool" in a clear fantasy setting. Even worse, players were supposed to carry the tool with them into the next room to use it, but since they didn't identify it as a tool they would often be lost for several minutes while trying to figure out how to even begin to play the next room.

Example of good puzzle design:

There was a key trapped in a series of pipes. Using bowls we had to carry water from a tub into the pipes until the key rose high enough for us to get it. What was even more fun was that there were holes in the pipe we had figure out how to plug by either using cork or our own hands.

Observational puzzles: luck and thought

Observational puzzles require special ways of looking at the environment or ways to manipulate the environment's visuals to put things in a new perspective. Like lateral puzzles, observation puzzles require luck and thought, but the luck component is more prominent. Players can usually immediately solve an observation puzzle if they look at the presented information from just to right angle or know exactly what to search for in the room.

Observation puzzles, being visually driven, are great opportunities for rooms to have big, flashy moments. Numbers written on a huge canvas, ping pong balls from firing pirate ships, or symbols paved into tile: observational puzzles can bring wonderful "larger than life" moments to your room. While it will only take a moment for players to "observe" your puzzles, that will be the moment they also most value your craftmanship.

Example of poor design:

A lot of observational puzzles use unique angles and player positions to achieve their effects. For example, you can only see numbers line up and sync together when standing in a particular place, otherwise they look scrambled. However, if it becomes too difficult to see the correct angle then the puzzle becomes frustrating. One of the most frustrating experiences I had was a puzzle in which you had to get on your hands and knees and then look at a 45-degree angle to see the correct projection. The room had a bit of signage to help direct the players, but it was an unnatural setup and we had to call in a hint to figure it out. Observational puzzles should be easy and direct points of room engagement that don't require a direct interaction with the Game Master.

Example of good design:

In one of my games the players activate the stage's curtain. Immediately the curtain pulls back to reveal a code written in five-foot letters on the canvas of a scene from Shakespeare's Romeo and Juliet. The funny thing is that the code is so large that sometimes players overlook it. But it's a great observation puzzle because it makes the code larger than life, just like you'd expect from the stage, haunted or no.

Player Participation Parameters

Your puzzle's participation parameters are how many people are required to solve the puzzle. Participation can be both essential, such as when one person must give commands while another person enacts them, or it can be optional, like a jigsaw puzzle that can be put together by multiple people working together to organize and place the pieces or only one dedicated person. Optional help can be organizing resources, reviewing gameplay strategies, or communicating information. Almost all rooms provide a method for writing down information so a player can store them for use in later puzzles. If they don't then an essential participation dynamic has been left out of the room.

2nd person player gameplay is one of the most unique and exciting aspects of IPE games and should definitely be emphasized in rooms, but a good game will have multiple participation parameters to keep up the variety of gameplay. A great room will have players want to run it again solely to play the puzzles from a different perspective and see what they missed.

The most important part about a puzzle's participation parameter is that they are clearly defined. If it is not immediately clear to everyone whether or not a puzzle requires multiple players than puzzle progression will be frustrating. I had a very fun puzzle in my room that has players operating elevator lifts to send a marble to the top of the tower. The problem is that players think the elevator controls are automatic so will put the marble in the first elevator over and over again waiting for something to happen. It is a standard part of the game experience now to let them know another player is required. We even have turned it into a game joke. I say, "perhaps there are elevator controls located on the other side?" Players then go to the other side and see "ELEVATOR CONTROLS!" written in bright red. It's even funnier because they've already interacted with the wall at that point and forgot about the large text they just saw. But the essential lesson is clear: if the controls don't clearly require two or more players then players will be confused by the interface.

One-player participation

One person participation is the standard puzzle participation experience that players can easily replicate at home, such as solving a riddle or code. Since no communication is required, teams will have to announce when the puzzle is solved and may end up confused on how much progress has been made in the room. Therefore it is always important to consider larger feedback moments when using these puzzles in a room, such as having the combination open a prominent chest.

One player games are great at giving us active verbs and helping us recapture primal hunting activities. You like to hunt creatures that have various skills and strengths. You aim at targets that have various speeds and durability. You control machines and processes, from falling blocks to combining groups. You surround, project, match, remember, and count. We capture, secure, fly, shoot, and fight. And the better the game, the better it adds a bit of role playing to the role. It can be as simple as making a matching game about matching colorful candy.

They mostly teach us our more primitive, but important behaviors. Hunting. Putting things in order. Gathering. Rescuing. Discovering the right combinations of actions is an important part of hunting as you learn the habits of your prey.

Two-player competition participation

Two player competition participation games are rarer in puzzle rooms because it is difficult to incorporate competition into story lines. Most two player competition games are tests of skill, speed, or knowledge.

Almost all two player games express themselves in physical activity: Shooting, bumping, racing, or ducking. This back and forth plays out in many different scenarios in rooms, from tossing a ball, to running a race, to even fighting imaginary villains. While harder to incorporate, competition games can still be a fun energy refresher in games because players will be more likely to recognize the style of gameplay then in other puzzles. The most important aspect to consider is a clear cue that players should engage in a competition. For example, two players may be invited the charge a device by pedaling two bicycles. The game will only progress if the players engage in the competition where someone clearly wins and someone clearly loses. The one that pedals faster will be declared the champion of the team and given a medal. While anyone can use the medal in a later puzzle, the faster peddler has still earned it at that moment and bragging rights for after the game.

Team participation

Classic team games are when two or more people have distinct roles necessary for completing the task. Most commonly existing in sports, team participation can also be used for controlling complex vehicles such as tanks, using industrial equipment, or artistic work such as performing on a stage. Team roles must be very clearly defined, however, to avoid organization chaos. Complicated goals often require complicated environments, and that can be overwhelming to players trying to process what they are seeing. It took me about 20 times to create a dancing puzzle that people could clearly understand and play, and I still have players that deeply struggle with it. But, for the ones that get it, helping their friends "learn" the dance move is the highlight of the room.

The IPE room takes advantage of the puzzle interface, however, to make team participation more fun than it could be in other environments. For example, a quarterback and a lineman cannot easily switch during a football game because their roles require unique training elements both physically and mentally. But in a puzzle environment, if the quarterback position is reduced to an easy "aiming" skill controlled by a tool and the lineman position is a simple blocking skill that requires no physical strength, the quarterback and the lineman can switch roles easily. It is not jumping into an "avatar" like in video games because no special personal training is required. Mastering a skill takes a minute and not a year.

Even video games are more difficult to share among friends as they usually require hand eye coordination or quick thinking skills that make it difficult to immediately grasp. But communication and teamwork are the most fun component of IPE games as the leadership and follower roles are defined and refined until the players win.

Supporting role participation

Supporting role participation games are games in which, while the game itself only really needs one player to be won, multiple people can take up roles to make it easier to solve. The game can either easily divide the necessary functions among multiple players or have one master player with others facilitating his gameplay. For example, if the players are playing a Simon like game, then multiple players can press different colors while one player writes down the sequence so they don't have to memorize it. Or, for a master player game, one person can work through a marble maze using a joystick to turn corners and try to avoid holes that the marble can drop through while the other players have buttons they can press to cover the holes and make it easier for the main player.

While the main player could finish the game entirely by herself, it is both easier and more fun to communicate with her teammates to have an easier experience and finish the challenge sooner. The most important thing is that the game could truly be accomplished (though would probably be too difficult to really be fun) by one player alone.

There are certain standard support roles in activities. The first is blocking. It is impossible to attack and defend yourself at the same time, so teammates will gather together to protect the person on the attack. This can translate into a lot of different gameplay scenarios as only one player will be able to progress with a puzzle while his teammates block distractions or obstacles. For example, one player may need to guide a ball up a maze but the enemy is shooting projectiles that will reset the maze if they strike it. The other players can gather together and protect the main player as he executes the puzzle.

Another standard support role is activation. If someone wants to jump rope with a large rope they will be unable to hold it on their own. They require supporters to hold and sway the rope. While the supporters no doubt have an easier job their job is still completely essential. This could be created in a game where the main player needs to fire an air gun at enemy ships while the supporting players charge it.

Finally, there is the support role of instruction. Supporting roles can give out instructions while the main player carries it out. The coach at a football game can be more aware of the situation than the players and so the orders he shouts out are essential to follow. Support players can see a pattern hidden from the main player that needs to carry it out. For example, they can see icons lit up that the main player will need to press. It is only by following instruction that the puzzle can be completed.

These types of game especially facilitate communication between players as the main player spends more time requesting help from the secondary players. The more that communication is encouraged in an IPE game, the better the experience for the group and the more unique the experience.

2nd Person perspective participation

2nd person gameplay participation relies on information and controls shared simultaneously by two players, but their roles can easily be switched and it is easy to express their needs. The most important difference between 2nd person gameplay and team gameplay is that players can never see each other in 2nd person gameplay and must communicate the necessary steps to each other. The "you" statements become essential to solving the puzzle where in team gameplay they are useful but optional.

These games make full use of the unique egalitarian quality of puzzle rooms, and that obstacles can exist in this environment that could not exist elsewhere. There is never going to be a pirate ship that has a wall split down the middle, for example, that requires the sailors to call out to each other what they are doing and should be doing. But it is easy to create these environments in an IPE game. 2nd person perspective gameplay rewards communication more than any other type of gameplay. I personally say take advantage of that fact and have at least one 2nd person perspective puzzle in each of your rooms!

Switching Player Participation

Not sure how to make a unique player participation game for your room? Well good news, any puzzle can have its player participation parameter changed. In fact, you shouldn't consider the player participation parameters until you have your planned set of puzzles for your room. Once you have them, you can imagine if they'd be more fun with the parameters changed and then decide on the final presentation of your puzzles for your game.

Consider the classic game of chess, one of the most prominent two-player competition games. Many rooms have already used chess as a one player participation puzzle: making the player perform one specific move to put the "opposition" in checkmate. When the piece is placed in the correct spot, the puzzle is solved. The largest part of the puzzle to solve is understanding the rules of chess enough to execute the correct placement.

Using chess as our template we can alter the participation parameters. Chess can become 2nd person player participation by introducing an avatar role. One player can see the board and the correct moves to win while another player "lives" it by stepping on the correct board squares. The avatar player, being inside the world, could see the pieces as true to life: real pawns, bishops, and knights that need to be fought against. The primary part of the puzzle becomes the communication between the two players to win the board game. Only the chess master player will know the correct path forward and only the avatar player can take it. The 2nd person player participation comes from the fact that these two roles can be easily switched if one of the players is having a more difficult time understanding how to identify the correct move or performing the actions to execute them.

One (+) participation is the same as normal chess, but divides up the functions if there are multiple players. The game could be played by just one person, put instead shifts and divides roles and puts different players in charge of different directions on the game board. One can move up, one to the side, etc. The nature of the game remains essentially the same as the one-player game, but the players share responsibility for making the correct moves.

Classic two player participation would be two people competing to finish a chess game first. For most puzzle games, this would be a game against a computer that was solving the same chess puzzle. If the computer wins first, then the puzzle would reset and the player would need to try again. If two people were competing against each other than the objective would become speed: both players working quickly so that one player officially wins and one player officially "loses" in a unique timeframe, such as completing an entire game in one minute's time. This would make the fun component playing the game as fast as possible, allowing players to even give each other tips on how to play faster. The competition aspect then changes to cooperative. They work together to compete better.

Team participation would be taking the basic roles of a chess game and using them on an actual battlefield: some people being able to move diagonally on squares and others straight, some a little and some a lot. This could be accomplished by creating vehicles programmed to move in certain directions as though they are actual chess pieces. Players would be working simultaneously as a group, but with the roles and rules of chess kept as a physical reality and challenge.

As you can see, changing how chess is used can make a simple puzzle into a completely dynamic team experience. Some parameters are better met by making the game more physical while some more mental, but all of them increase the need for communication and quick thinking to make the room more fun.

Puzzle Value

Now that you have your puzzles and their participation parameters set it is time to decide on their best value in the room. Like player participation, puzzle values can be changed and scaled up or scaled down. You can increase the complexity of the interface, the dimensions of the puzzle, and the special effects used in the puzzle. Puzzles get their value rating both from active and passive gameplay. This includes the difficulty of their set-up, the intensity of their usage, and the length of time required to reset them between games. The more players are readily able to tell that love has been put into the puzzle's creation and maintenance, the more they will appreciate the experience even if the puzzle isn't their favorite type. However, for players to properly appreciate a highly valued puzzle moment they will also need to experience small puzzle moments in the game too. You don't appreciate the spectacular play of a touchdown without also seeing simpler pass and run plays.

Each value name will be matched to the attraction value name already used in theme parks: The A-E ticket system. Pioneered by Disney, A tickets are for the cheapest rides and E tickets the most expensive ones. In the early days of Disneyland, guests would be issued booklets with more A tickets than E tickets in order to control the crowd but, as Disney grew, they abandoned the system. People wanted the freedom to ride the E ticket attractions over and over again without buying new booklets. Given that the parks are stuffed full of people, this lowered the quality of the crowd control in Disney. Luckily, IPE rooms can provide the perfect crowd control by offering puzzles exclusively to private group after private group. This new ability to pace the entertainment makes planning the perfect puzzle value ratio much easier for designers, especially designers that really like a challenge!

This section of the book will examine samples from the different styles of puzzles and how they build from freebie attractions to impressive "E" tickets. The examples will go through various standard puzzle environments to better illustrate how the puzzles shift and build their values from simple usages of puzzles to astounding show stoppers.

Freebies

In theme parks, "Freebies" are the atmospheric vehicles that move us to the attractions themselves: the trains and people movers that describe the world and its history as they take us to a more exciting roller coaster. They don't cost a ticket to ride and while still part of the "regular world" they better prep us for the fantastic situations we are about to enjoy. Typically, they will have no wait time to board the vehicles and are used for their convenience, but without these rides we'd feel less drawn into the special world. There is a difference between riding the family mini-van to the park and riding a special open-air train that foretells exciting adventure to come. Guests won't think of taking pictures of these attractions but they will know they are leaving the everyday.

In zoos, where vehicles are a much less common part of the experience, they are the pictures and posters of the animals that teach you about their habits and better prepare you for seeing the animals themselves. Without the signs explaining what you are about to see could easily be seen on your computer screen at home, knowing they are about to introduce you to the real animals is an exciting departure from the everyday.

In IPEs, freebies are the puzzles that are so quick and easy to solve that they are more like atmospheric elements in the room. They are also the clues discovered by players when they search the room. In most rooms today, they are the first puzzle players will encounter, like a character's name being a lock code or searching the room for a semi-hidden key. This gets people excited to play the game in earnest and start working on the harder puzzles they will soon encounter. They introduce us to the world and help us depart from the everyday.

Freebies are all about intriguing the mind and wanting the player to crave additional experiences and successes. They are simultaneously a welcome, a way to tell backstory, and the last reminder of the everyday before entering a world exclusively made of magic. Outside of a room, playing a freebie puzzle would not be a very convincing show of just why an IPE games are so much fun. The actions of a freebie puzzle translate too well into everyday actions. Similarly, receiving clues outside of the game experience is much less fun for players. Discovering them hidden inside the world is always more exciting.

Arcade Puzzle Example

An easy physical action that requires no practice or skill but still requires physical interaction. In a haunted house game, players could see a portrait that covers up part of a message. "Beware you..." When they take down the portrait they see the rest of the message. "...are in great danger!" By moving furniture players feel greater control over the choices they will be making.

Assemble Puzzle Example

This puzzle will have a straightforward and quick assembly with no possibility of needing to sort multiple pieces or assemble the item incorrectly. In a space game, your team would need to use a space portal in order to stop an attacking alien force. By putting together a specific symbol you can fire up the portal gate and leap into a distant quadrant. The symbol itself is four pieces that can be put into the correct shape following their outline on top of the device. It only takes a moment to assemble but gives you complete power over the portal.

Code Puzzle Example

This will be the most simplistic code available to the players: a two to four option code. The code can be entered using switches or arrows that are easy to follow (such as left/right or up/down options). The code will be straightforward and not require a process to be solved (such as using equations or a cipher) and could easily be memorized by the player. These are codes that are able to be uncovered through observation alone. For example, when your group tries to enter a medieval castle you need to figure the correct up or down position of several levers by the gate door. You see a row of knights to the side of the door that seem strange, some looking up and some looking down. Using their positions as the code, you are able to pull the levers into the correct position and open the door. Given that it is only a two-option code, your group might even be able to guess the answer simply by experimenting with up and down positions from the levers, given that there would be a low total of possible positions to try.

Experimental Puzzle example

This would be any experimental puzzle with a small number of possible attempts before a clear success will be achieved. Players would also use an interface that they would already be familiar with, such as searching through multiple keys on a ring or trying to find a particular radio station without knowing the exact station number. For example, the team is trapped in a pirate ship's dungeon. Luckily, a mysterious friend has slipped you a ring of keys through the porthole window of your prison. You experiment with the different keys in the dungeon's lock until you are finally able to open the door and enter the ship's hold.

Lateral thinking puzzle

The puzzle uses observation and pattern recognition as the chief principle of discovering the leap of logic. Players can match strange objects together due to a clear matching pattern they share. For example, in an Egypt game, examining the pharaoh's signet ring given to you by a previous explorer, you notice that the pattern on the ring matches the pattern on the middle of a door that leads to the pharaoh's inner chambers. Under the pattern is a small indention that just might fit the ring. Pressing the ring into it, the door rumbles away, allowing you access inside.

Maze puzzle example

The puzzle will use the basic maze style that players will recognize from solving puzzle games and books. For example, to enter the forbidden temple, first you need to solve the labyrinth on a pedestal by the front door. The key to the door is in the center of the maze and must be guided to the maze's exit. Once you successfully retrieve the key from the labyrinth you can enter the temple.

Observational Puzzle Example

This puzzle could link the same visual clue between two objects that have an easily recognized association between them, like the luggage identification tags people use in order to find their bags among others at an airport. For example, in a murder mystery game, you are invited by the detective to solve the murder of a man upon an express train. First, you must open his luggage to get further clues as to what he was doing there, but you are not sure which bag is his. Luckily, you notice among the available bags is one with a picture of a Labradoodle. As the man was a dog breeder, you know that this is his luggage case and you can retrieve it to begin to solve the mystery.

Tool Puzzle Example

The puzzle requires the use of a well-known tool that is easy to use and there are no special environmental needs required to use it. Players will probably have already interacted with this tool in everyday life and even if it is a retro technology (such as a radio) it is very clear how to operate it and has labels such as "Power," "Tune," "FM/AM." If players were spies on a secret mission, they might need to turn on a special radio that will give you the secret message from spy headquarters for your mission. They would quickly know where to set it to if given a message say "89 FM."

Sensory Puzzle Example

Feel is the easiest sense to use for identification and can be used for distinct, everyday objects such as toys or fruit. In a fantasy game, say you have an assortment of fruit in front of you, but which is the fairy favorite? Only the correct gift will tempt the fairies into opening the tree door to the fairy forest. Reaching into the whispering grasses, you feel the shape of grapes. Knowing that, you select grapes as your gift and the tree door blossoms open.

Game Puzzle example

This puzzle would use a simple version of an existing popular game that is probably already well known by the players and which has simple rules. Additionally, there would be only a few possible moves and pieces for the players to use to complete the puzzle. As an example, a serial killer has locked you in his basement and is treating you as his chess pawns. To symbolize this, he has you play a game of chess and move the queen to checkmate the king. The second you move the queen into the checkmate position, a hammer comes down, smashing the king piece and revealing a key inside.

A ticket

"A" ticket values are rides with small wait times, like mini roller coasters for children or basic thrill rides that spin your vehicle around. These rides are less intense because they are made for younger audiences and are more straightforward in their design. These rides are great in the theme park when you want a break from a more intense ride. They can be colorful, but don't have elaborate stories or special effects associated with them. Guests won't be very tempted to take pictures of their experience.

For zoos, it is seeing the environments of animals but not seeing the animals themselves. While seeing the environments can be intriguing and is unique to the zoo, you're missing out on the action you really came for and so will lose interest quickly.

An "A" ticket puzzle should engage the players and be a great confidence boost for beginning players but still fun for experienced players. It could be used to describe what makes a puzzle environment unique but would probably be overruled by better examples. It's a good pause between more complicated puzzles that require more teammates or more brain power.

Arcade puzzle example

The puzzle is a small midway game or incorporates midway action elements when being solved. The puzzle's physical activity might take a few attempts to master but is still a simple straightforward action. For example, in the forbidden temple you must shoot a ball into an idol's mouth. The idol needs to be "fed" so that it will let you pass. The idol is behind bars so that the ball cannot simply be placed into his mouth and the floor slopes so the ball can roll back to you if you miss your shot and need to try again. Given an obvious arcade set-up players should recognize the challenge fairly quickly and make the shot within a few attempts.

Assemble puzzle example

The puzzle requires more direct interaction with the environment and can either require simple sorting of numerous pieces or the assembly of several distinct objects. What is being assembled has common real-life examples already in the mind of the players, either the pieces of an object or the picture of a standard jigsaw puzzle. For example, you come across the crumbled statues of the family that used to own a haunted mansion. By reassembling them, the spirits of that tragic family will appear before you and invite you to learn their torturous history for yourself.

Code Puzzle example

This will be a more complicated code with two to six options. The code can be given through instructions that may also need to be deciphered by the team. For example, the train's power must be turned back on for the players to continue their murder investigation. Following the engineer's instructions will give them the method they need, but they are in shorthand. The players will decipher "FWD" means "forward" and "P Red B" means "Press Red Button" and so on until they can turn on the train.

Experimental Puzzle example

Players must experiment to input a three-step sequence. For example, you need to press a series of buttons in the correct order and if you press the wrong button the machine automatically resets and you have to try and press the entire sequence again from the beginning. This could be used in a spy game where your spy crew must press the correct buttons in order to complete a hacking sequence. You guess until all the buttons light up and you're inside the main frame.

Lateral thinking puzzle example

A higher-level lateral thinking puzzle uses more complex observation. Players might need to look through multiple distortions, different planes of vision, or see things in a very unusual way. A hint in the environment might be required, like if players need to stand in a specific place to connect all the dots in front of them. For example, in the fantasy game, to better understand how to use the fairy portals, you need to look through them and understand how to properly view their distorted features. From the correct angle, the portal reveals how to read the language of the fairies by shifting around the letters on the page right before your eyes (this can be accomplished through a color filter effect or through polarization).

Maze Puzzle example

A maze that serves a dual purpose, such as collecting items in various corners of the maze or slowly uncovering a code answer. The maze stops being just about finding the correct route and more about actively exploring or solving a mystery about it. For example, in the pirate game, you retrieve a maze tablet from untangled vines that has distinct island symbols in various corners of the maze. By tracing the correct route through the maze, you run over five specific symbols. Remembering these symbols and their sequence gives you the code to open a chest in the captain's quarters.

Observational Puzzle example

The puzzle requires players to understand the orientation of objects in the environment. For instance, players first realize that something is "off" about a pattern of objects and then figure out the deeper meaning behind the irregularity. In the sci-fi game, as you are examining the planet charts of your spaceship, you notice that certain planets start shimmering under the navigation's spotlight. You realize that they form a constellation that will take you to the secret alien galaxy and put in the coordinates.

Tool Puzzle example

A tool that can take a bit of time to understand how to use in the environment. There is still a clear need in the environment that can be explored by the players to figure out how the tool works. The tool is easy to use and requires no particularly special set-up once you solve the particular use for it. For example, inside the Medieval castle your team looks up and realizes that a key is hanging from the chandelier. You take the spear from one of the knight statues lining the hall and use it to fetch the key from the chandelier by hooking it onto the spear and fetching it.

Sensory Puzzle example

The puzzles are still sensory in nature but use more challenging feel patterns with more ambiguous shapes for the players to decipher with their hands. In the serial killer game, the killer has you feel through the holes in a wall and touch all the tools he uses to commit his crimes as well as some of his favorite body parts. Your only guide to what you are seeing is the insane notebook sketches he uses to scribble down his ideas. You use a corresponding number code that matches up to some of his tools and parts to open his toolbox.

Game Puzzle example

The puzzle has a more complex setup with more possible gameplay movements and rules. This could be a game of scrabble with specific words that need to be completed by the player, or a pyramid math puzzle. For example, in the Egypt game, to prove your worth as a possible servant of the pharaoh, you must use the eternal math of the ancients to place sequential numbers of the pyramid in the correct order. Doing so correctly will highlight certain numbers and gives you the Egyptian engineer's code.

B ticket

With "B" tickets guests start to get introduced to more exciting themes and experiences. In theme parks, these would be vehicle rides in which you have control over your own vehicle on a mini track, such as go carts. They are also the more high-end thrill rides, such as the pirate ship that swings back and forth, and will have more exciting components or more extensive theming, such as extensive lighting or characters associated with the ride. These rides will have a low to medium wait. Guests will be more tempted to take a picture of the experience, but at most just one photo and less likely to share that picture with other people.

For zoos, it is finally seeing the animals. While the animals may not be doing anything more than sleeping in their environments, you have still achieved the main goal of coming to a zoo and so have had a successful experience. You'll finally have something to tell your friends about the day.

Similarly, a "B" puzzle is a complete experience that satisfies the basic desires of the players that are paying to experience a game. It starts to showcase what your environment is all about and the unique fun that only exists in a puzzle room. It would not be enough for players all on its own but does help them appreciate the unique nature of their fun.

Arcade Puzzle example

At this point the arcade puzzle is a normal sized midway game. More careful movement is required, there will probably be more attempts needed to win, and there could be more complex mechanics to navigate. A good example is a patience game, in which you must carefully move a wire from one end of the machine to another. Failing to do so causes the game to reset. In the sci-fi game, to accomplish your trek through the stars, you must steer towards a "B" class planet. You have to be very careful with the controls because one wrong move will cause the planet's "negative" gravity to push your ship backwards and require you to try and land all over again. You must navigate the one specific path and avoid the borders on each side.

Assemble Puzzle Example

The puzzles now become more unique, incorporating custom design so that the items being assembled are unique to the game world and would never be assembled in real life. The puzzle will also start requiring specialized technology, such as RFID tags to confirm their proper placement of pieces as the assembling itself would not trigger an effect naturally. For example, the serial killer's book collection has unique jacket covers that can be assembled into a specific design painted by the killer. Assembling the books in their proper places on his shelf will immediately unlock a secret wall and let you explore more of his dungeon. The only way the system knows the books are in the correct order is because each has an RFID tag and is read by the system.

Code Puzzle example

A four to nine option code that can be entered into standard numeric pads. For the players to find out the necessary code they will need to tackle more complicated processes, like using assemble aspects. The code will be complex enough that it will almost certainly need to be written down by the players in order to be successfully entered. For example, in the spy game, your supercomputer gadget has been able to hack into the enemy's main frame, and it is able to print out all the sequences used by the staff to gain access to the safe. By tracing out the common component in each staff's sequence you are able to stitch them all together into one master override code. You input the master code sequence which is 12-steps long.

Experimental Puzzle example

At this level an assembly component can be added to the experimentation such as trying different combinations of pieces to see if they work. You can also check two different series of objects and see how they connect with each other. For the designer, it becomes more important to confirm that the amount of variables do not become overwhelming to the player and that they still enjoy experimenting with the objects. As an example, in the haunted house game, to get the elevator working you open the back panel and see a complicated series of levers and gears. Working with different combinations of them, you can get the elevator working again.

Lateral thinking puzzle example

The lateral thinking requires players to understand code puzzle type elements but with very unique or strange components. The equation language can use arcane symbols or, conversely, everyday objects. Simple equations or already translated phrases can be introduced into the environment to help players make the required leap in thinking. For example, in the forbidden temple game, as you are studying the positions of a row of idols, you realize you can translate their specific posture into numbers and "+" and "-" symbols. Writing it down, you can solve an equation and put the last idol in the position of the answer, unlocking a new secret portion of the temple.

Maze puzzle example

The maze starts to use particularly unique mechanics, such as it is mounted to be vertical on a wall or has multiple levels that a marble must travel through. For example, the Egypt game could have a maze with multiple chambers forming a mini pyramid. You have to roll a marble from the top to the bottom.

Observational Puzzle example

Players will need to recognize the special classification of a series of objects in the room. This will typically be given to the players with code or tool puzzle components. To properly find the objects first may require learning exactly how to spot them in the environment. For the designer, organically incorporating the objects into the environment will require a more robust design and set-up than typical of puzzles but having observational puzzles deeply tied to the environment is more fun for players. In the pirate game, out of the many knots on the rigging of a pirate ship, only five are the correct knots used for the captain's number code. By searching the ship and finding the knots among the ropes you are able to count the correct numbers hidden on them and open the door to the captain's room.

Tool Puzzle example

For players to use the tool they must also alter the environment in a special way. Whatever the effect chosen, the environment will be permanently changed. This requires double duty for the designer as they must prepare both the reaction of the tool from the puzzle but also the reaction of the special effect on the environment. In the fantasy example, players must use the special midnight sun of the forest to repair the fairy's village. By using a special stick, the dark light shines on different sections of village and repairs the houses. The houses will then remain repaired for the rest of the game.

Sensory Puzzle example

For this sense puzzle, players will be hearing or producing sounds. Sounds can be more readily confused and require greater set up by the designer to play in the environment. For example, in the murder mystery the detective gives you the interview tapes he made of the suspects. By playing the witness recordings you can learn more about the people on the train and their alibis for the time of the murder. Hearing their statements directly helps you solve the murder.

Game Puzzle example

The games become more advanced and could require more pieces that are permanently attached to the equipment or can be interacted with in multiple ways. For designers, these puzzles will require a PLC

("Programmable Logic Controller") and multiple sensors to track the player's progress. In the medieval castle game, there is a special display of mosaics in a stained-glass window that can be manipulated by being slid by the player. When the mosaic is correctly assembled, the bricks behind it crumble to reveal the secret crown of the king (PLC confirms when all the pieces are in place and releases the bricks through magnetic sensors).

C ticket

"C ticket" rides are the storybook dark rides that are especially exciting to children. These are the smaller roller coasters that are fun for beginners, such as wooden coasters. These rides are where the truly special memories begin to be made, like the "it's a small world" ride in Disney World. Whenever people think of cheery music and endless rows of dancing dolls, they will always remember that ride because there is nothing else like it in the world. Guests are more likely to take pictures and may even take multiple pictures of the ride if they really connect to it. They also may want to talk about it to other people.

For zoos, guests have a chance to see multiple animals at once on a zoo ride, be it on a jeep or a train. This gives them their first experience not just seeing the animals but interacting with the staff as well as they listen to the explanations of what they are seeing. Being on a ride, they are ensured special sights of the animal.

A "C ticket" puzzle should be exciting to the players and give them a thrill from solving it. The puzzle should be so interesting that the player would want to solve it again to share the experience with friends. On its own, it would be naturally attractive to people and call attention to itself so that even people who aren't into puzzles would want to interact with it.

Arcade Puzzle example

The arcade puzzle is an oversized and specially presented midway game. The game has more reactions as it is played and even changes states. For the designer, this means multiple stages of lighting, movement, and sound and special PLC requirements. The serial killer invites you to play a midway game made entirely of body parts, a classic "use the hammer to flip parts into the center" game but using body parts for the flipping. As you play, each body part has its own squishy sound effect, just to really drive him the grossness. Winning his game earns you more respect and lets you into his secret lair.

Assemble Puzzle example

This puzzle combines observation principles with assembly principles and uses surprising effects, especially optical illusions and special lights, in the puzzle. For the pirate game, you retrieve treasures from the pirates that seem random at first, but when assembled on the captain's table in the correct way and shown in a special light, they reveal a secret code of numbers in their combined shadows.

Code Puzzle example

The code interface can have beyond nine options and even use an entire grid. The code can now be discovered by using tools, such as a cipher, the most common specialized tool for solving codes. The more unique and interesting the tool used the better, as simple paper ciphers are easy to use and common in paper puzzles. A complicated mechanical cipher would be more fun for players. For example, in the Egypt game, by placing the eye of Ra into the beam of sunlight, the eye acts as a prism and highlights the exact symbols you need for a code.

Experimental Puzzle example

In larger ticket cases, the experiment elements remain isolated but take on more theatrical effects in their experimentation. They require more physical activity and have more permanent physical consequences to the room when it is solved. While experimenting with the puzzle, bigger reactions and effects can be made for failed attempts. In the forbidden temple game, pulling the right vines above the players can break apart the door holding them back. When the three correct vines are pulled in the correct places the door will collapse. Attempting to pull more than three vines at once will reveal the bones of unlucky adventures who tried to conquer the vines before you.

Lateral thinking puzzle example

The lateral thinking puzzle will now use maze mechanics in its construction. Such as having a surprising maze layout or optics in the maze itself. In the sci-fi game, the players encounter a strange maze system during their planetary exploration. The planet has strange rules unique from the normal expectation of movement (down on the controls makes the players turn left, pressing a button makes them move forward, etc.) so as the players control their way through the maze they have to learn the special way to proceed.

Maze Puzzle example

The maze starts to have game elements built into it, such as time limits or particular rules of play. The game elements also open up the ability for the designer to add more special effects to the maze gameplay. In the haunted house game, in order to connect the ghost equipment to the environment the players must set it all up with a time limit. This is done by guiding a controller through a unique environmental maze.

Failing to set it up properly has the environment "shift" to new parameters and the players must start over.

Observational Puzzle example

The puzzle uses unique objects that have a noticeable mistake or absence among them. The observation requires you to understand the difference between the normal form and the abnormal form of objects. For example, in the spy game, one of your team's contacts deliberately made mistakes in the creation of art in a gallery. If the team finds the mistakes, then they will get a special message that will help them fight their enemies.

Tool Puzzle example

Use a unique tool with fun and surprising characteristics that are transformative. The players need to start by understanding how the tool works before using it. In the murder mystery, the team must get to the roof of the train with a retractable ladder. The killer hid the murder weapon on the top of the train and it has to be manually retrieved by the ladder.

Sensory Puzzle example

This puzzle uses balance on objects. Using the sense of balance can help players discover a secret structure or weigh different objects. In the medieval game, players prove themselves worthy of entering the castle's blacksmith room by balancing the correct weight of bricks in a trough. They need to strike the right balance with the bricks gained through the game. They need to pair the bricks by the same weights to stack them properly.

Game Puzzle Example

The game now involves an instrument. Either a musical instrument or a simplified version of a well-known machine. There are rules and goals that must be completed when using the device. In the fantasy example, players now summon the spirits of the forest by using fairy instruments to play the correct tune.

D ticket

"D" tickets are the high-level dark rides that push their concepts to exciting new heights, such as the "Peter Pan Ride" in Disney World. While the Peter Pan model is still a track ride, since the track is on top and not on the bottom you are able to pass by model sets of incredible intensity. The unique construction gives riders the ability to weave in and out of them and feels even more incredible when you fly over an entire pirate ship.

Roller Coasters are the main "D ticket" attraction for theme parks. While roller coasters are the undisputed king of straightforward presentations, those presentations always deliver on their promises of great heights, sudden drops, and exciting twists and reversals. When you ride a roller coaster you get exactly the thrills you expected because you could see them beforehand as other riders screamed past you at high speeds. For these rides, players are likely to take multiple pictures or even pay for a souvenir picture of the experience that proved they were there. They are even likely to take a video of themselves enjoying the experience.

For zoos, this is giving people the dream of interacting with the animals on an individual level: being able to touch, pet, and feed them. Interacting with animals on this level truly makes them feel alive to the patron.

These are the flagship attractions that get people to commit to the experience: what they see on the poster and what is at the top of their list to experience. It is the moment that would get their friends to commit to coming to the game.

Outside of the game, this puzzle would attract people and have them be willing to pay for the experience of playing it. The puzzle should fulfill every expectation of the experience the player was imaging when they purchased the game, from large props to exciting mechanics. This is the movie moment that the players wanted to experience and will have the team talking about the room after playing it.

Arcade Puzzle Example

Players need to master and maneuver an independent vehicle in the environment to win. More complicated mechanics require for both controlling the vehicle and using it in the environment. For example, in the pirate game, now that the players have escaped the pirate ship, they must use a boat to get to the desert island. Figuring out how to control the boat and use the oars and rudder has them pushing through the waves on to the island to dig up the treasure.

Assemble Puzzle example

Players must assemble an entire mini-environment for the puzzle, such as a model or a track. Assembling forms of movement is one of the greatest and most fun challenges of design and can be an exciting activity to share with players because it gives them a high feeling of control as they watch the motion they have created come to life. For example, in the forbidden temple game, to retrieve the temple's gems, players must assemble a minecar track. Once it is correctly assembled, they can use a mine train to collect the gems they need. Players can use the assembled track to travel to other areas of the temple. For example, the designer can set up closed circuit control cameras that display models of other temple rooms.

Code Puzzle example

Code can have multiple interfaces that are connected by players using tools. They can also use the integration of sense puzzles for the code, including more complicated observational set-ups. In the haunted house game, there are certain echoes through the house that you need to translate into your audio equipment. First you capture the echoes, then you find the right translation of them to retrieve the code to the grandfather's chest.

Experimental Puzzle example

Players must now experiment using entire machines and equipment. Experimentation requires use of multiple tools and interfaces to understand and engage the environment. In the sci-fi game, the players must now learn how to use the navigation, weapons, and shield controls of the starship by trial and error before they are able to fight the evil starship. In the training environment, they can learn how to move in multiple directions, how to target and shoot, and how to charge the shields to protect themselves.

Lateral thinking puzzle example

The lateral thinking now extends to using strange tools or Rube Goldberg style devices in order to accomplish a required goal. For example, in the fantasy game, the fairies need you to use the magical tools of the forest to fight off the construction workers. By using the magical tool that extends the roots of trees you can push the vehicles away and block them from entering the forest.

Maze Puzzle example

Special tools are used to control the maze's environment or guide movement in the maze. The puzzle combines tools and environmental learning as well as the usual maze puzzle of finding the correct path. Note that these tools could be used for more than moving through the maze but can also interact with the game elements, such as having the tool create special effects with its use. In the serial killer game, the killer has tools to control his maze. The different tools of the serial killer are needed to control your way through the maze until you find him. As you use the tools, different victim body parts and routes open in the maze for you to navigate.

Observational Puzzle example

Use a puzzle that incorporates changing colors and lights as players interact with it. A high-ticket observation puzzle is more expensive to set up and basically overpowers the other puzzles in the environment when it is active by drawing a lot of player attention. A great high level observational puzzle is something players won't want to miss. In the medieval game, you are able to adjust the stained-glass windows to make the lights and colors match the royal banners on the wall. When the stained glass windows are correctly aligned, the royal guard will be summoned and will give you the weapons you need to fight the dragon.

Tool Puzzle example

The players use a tool in a way that alters the environment in innovative ways. These are when the tools the players are using match the tools used by heroes in movies. Their use can affect the environment in surprising ways and use special effects to seem especially powerful. In the Egypt game, the inner chamber to the pharaoh's tomb can only be accessed by using a claw over the tomb's skylight and then pulling off the bars blocking the door. The designer has to use behind-the-scenes magic to make this happen, such as guiding the claw with magnets so that it automatically clicks into the correct place to pull against the bars as well as having the bars look heavy but actually be lightweight foam so that the players can easily move them.

Sensory Puzzle example

Players now must smell the correct scents in order to solve a puzzle. The control of smells is more difficult to manage and usually requires a neutral smell for resetting. In the spy game, combining the right smells creates a knockout gas. This will cause the spy headquarter guards all to fall asleep and give you a chance to access the master computer.

Game Puzzle example

A game in which the choices the players make has an automatic feedback response from the system. This is how most video games are played and fits everything from a "lights out" game to a game with rotating pieces or moveable avatars. Playing a mini-computer game in a real environment can be difficult for players to comprehend as it can be more of an interface than they are expecting but can also be some of the coolest player moments if done well. In the murder mystery game, you must open the suitcase of the eccentric inventor, but it has a strange lock that mirrors your movements in a mini-maze. You must move your maze piece while also tracking the other piece's independent movements. As you work through the maze, the two pieces finally meet up in the middle and the suitcase opens up, giving you the last clues you need to solve the mystery.

E ticket

The "E ticket" is the highest attraction rating and is the true show stopper. These experiences are events that guests had no idea was even possible and exceed any possible expectation they could have had. It's not the amateur dreams of customers but professionals who devote their time to finding the best puzzle experiences. While everyone is able to imagine exciting moments to a certain extent, the best moments can only be created by a true master, like a chef who knows how to create a presentation out of food that surpasses flavor alone.

These are the theme park rides that use hybrid elements from multiple rides. One of the best examples is the Universal Studios "Spider Man" ride, that uses 3d glasses in a dark ride environment to make it seamlessly feel like you're soaring through the air and battling super villains in the streets of New York. Or the "Harry Potter" ride that includes roller coaster aspects with heavy theming to make you feel like you're darting past spiders and flying on the quidditch team. When different technology is combined in rides, the unique possibilities become astounding. Guests will want to take pictures and videos but know they can never truly capture the amazing experience. So instead they'll buy souvenirs or t-shirts to commemorate the experience.

For zoos, this is a higher level of interaction that requires training and preparation before the patrons can interact with the animals, such as swimming with dolphins or going on a safari inside of the park. These are VIP experiences that people pay extra for: the experiences that even have elements of mild danger that require staff supervision.

The key to "E ticket" experiences is that they always have the ability to surprise guests and be unpredictable. These are the moments that the entire show can be built around and will sometimes take more months of planning and construction than every other moment of the game combined. They are our deepest moments of fantasy and could be the entire experience itself if the rest of the puzzles weren't so fun. Given their intensity, they should either be at the end of the game or require a major tonal shift in the game experience so that players aren't disappointed in new puzzle experiences after playing them.

This is a puzzle that the player would pay just for a chance to repeat it, because the experience is so incredible. Having "E" puzzles makes players advocates of your room, telling others to go and experience the room for themselves.

Arcade Puzzle Example

Tackling a huge challenge using arcade maneuvers that mimics action hero movies. You need to duck and fly, toss and defend etc. and use to save the day. For example, at the conclusion of the medieval game now that the players have secured all the weapons they are ready to attack the dragon that is attacking the castle. It will require all of their skills as they block his breaths of fire and toss spears into his weak points. Design wise, the controls must recognize that they have "defended" themselves against harmless smoke and orange and red lights before the dragon opens up his weak point and gives them a chance to throw the game-winning spear.

Assemble Puzzle example

The puzzle requires them to assemble a scenario or a story. They are not just crafting an environment, but the idealized state of an environment in which a story will play out. In the ending of the murder mystery game, it is time to solve the case, and players can prove who the killer is by putting together the evidence of the crime. They assemble the movie of how the crime went down using props and tools. When everything comes together the crime again plays out and the theory is proved correct. If their theory is incorrect than the movie displays where it breaks down, such as not being able to prove the selected killer actually had a motive.

Code Puzzle example

The code itself is a series of mini-games that must be solved. The code in this case becomes more of a theme than an actual code but it ties all the mini-games together. For example, at the end of the pirate game the players fight against the pirate king by competing in a series of challenges. After they win each challenge they receive a colored gem. Placing all the gems into the pirate's treasure chest gives them the right to retrieve his treasure.

Experimental Puzzle example

The puzzle requires players to interact with characters themselves to solve it. The most extensive and fun style of experimentation is working with people because they can have the most surprising reactions to your interactions, such as eagerly accepting a bribe or becoming deeply insulted by an attempt at bribery. In the end of the fairy game, the players gather the fairies and lead them in a final battle. They figure out what is required to motivate each of them and then work together to save the forest from destruction once and for all.

Lateral thinking puzzle example

The puzzle uses an entire game with strange, unique thinking. The game has uncommon logic and surprising rules, in which half the time is spent understanding how the game works and how to win it. In the serial killer game, it would be one final crazy game against the serial killer himself. Players figure out his rules of madness because in this final game it will be "kill or be killed."

Maze Puzzle example

The maze incorporates advanced arcade elements, such as the use of vehicles or games of chance, in order to be completed. In the end of the sci-fi game, players navigate through the final maze while protecting their ship from enemy fighters so they can fire the bomb through the ventilation vents that will destroy the evil mothership.

Observational Puzzle example

The puzzle uses lights that involve optical illusions. These puzzles will require complicated and specialized equipment to be used, but will also be the most exciting for players to interact with in the game environment, using elements such as snow, lasers, and mirror effects. For example, in the forbidden temple game you use the spirits of the temple to retrieve the golden eye of the idol. As the temple breaks down around you, the directions of light and optical illusions will help you "trap" the idol in another dimension and retrieve the ultimate prize.

Tool puzzle example

The puzzles use fantasy tools that are the ultimate in movie props and greatly change the environment in astounding ways. In the haunted house game, these are the tools the players use to exorcise the ghosts from the haunted house for good. They channel the spirits into various ghost traps to complete their "unfinished business" and free them for good.

Sensory Puzzle example

The puzzle requires tasting objects. Tasting will always be the most impressive use of senses because it requires a complicated reset for your guests as well as unique storage requirements such as refrigeration or warming drawers. In the Egypt game, players eat the Egyptian delights of the inner chamber and discover the true tastes of the pharaoh. Only then will they deserve the rewards of the Egyptian gods. By matching each of the treats to the proper spice they are able to prove their refined taste.

Game Puzzle example

A game against a competitor, whether the game master is controlling the interface behind the scenes or with a computer program. For example, in the end of the spy game, players break into the final computer and must use all their hacking skills to play a game of "connect four" (secretly against the game master) to win control of the entire system.

Clue Language

In rooms, there is a completely distinct language for the players delivered in the medium of clues. The most important aspect to remember about clues is that they will exist for every group. While some groups need specific nudges or open-ended statements to have a great time in your environment, the clues will always be available for every game even though they might only appear at certain times or still be specifically activated by the game master. Active clues are clues that your players absolutely will see during the course of the game and passive clues are clues that the players may see. Every player will see a big sign that says "Danger! Do not touch the red block!" but players might miss a clue hidden behind a curtain that says, 'Do not touch the red block." The great thing about having passive clues in your environment is that it gives the game host or master another element to point to before having to engage in a more possibly game-breaking statement to the players.

There are many different ways to express clues in your environment, and the more ways you do, the more fun your players will have finding them and using them to solve puzzles. Besides solving the puzzles directly, the other main activity for players will be gathering clues about what to do next, so a great variety of clues makes for a great game. The last avenue for clues should be calling the game master, not the first. Having a variety of clues for every puzzle makes your team communicate more with each other as well as protects the idea that they are truly the heroes of the world. Heroes notice the subtle signs that everyone else misses and don't need to depend on backup for answers.

Instructions

Instructions can be given for certain puzzle elements and interfaces, especially if it would make sense to have instructions for equipment in the real world. It is important that instructions be as brief as possible, however, as groups don't like to be bogged down by reading while playing a game. For example, you do not have to include "world making" elements in your instructions, such as explaining how each of the puzzle pieces organically fit in the world. Make the instructions as brief as possible while respecting the language design element of your world.

For example "Mr. Maze's Amazing potion is mixed as follows: 1 part blue, 3 parts red, and 2 parts green. Use the correct sized pots or the potion will fizzle!" delivers a clear set of instructions to the player. Compare it to the following: "Mr. Maze's Amazing potion is just what you need to cure your everyday cold! Using your wizard training, carefully mix 1 parts artic blue, 3 parts lava red, and 2 parts forbidden forest green. We have specifically sourced pots from the mountains of Tarvana. You must judge for yourself the best possible pot or the potion will only be good for Mrs. Fuzzlebottom's imps!"

The second set of instructions is a lot more playful and provocative. And players will not understand a word of it. Trust me: I'd love for players to appreciate colorful commentary in a game. But that is rarely the reality of an IPE.

Advertisements

Almost all environments have advertisement elements, and ads are a great way to introduce information to players. After all, ads are always trying to teach you something in order to sell you something. Using these teaching moments to introduce concepts to players is a great way to engage them. For example, "Stand here to enjoy the unique sites of Haunted Mountain! Brought to you by the tourism board of Haunted Mountain" is a great way to draw players to an observation puzzle without breaking the reality of the game.

Lights

Turning on lights to highlight certain parts of the room is a great way to bring focus to players about what to do next or how to use a tool. As they play the game and spotlights cycle through the experience, it also gives players a real sense of progression and impact. The game master will turn on the lights when it is appropriate to do so which means some players may never encounter them, but they still count as a clue because they must be hard wired into the system before the game starts. When I point out a specific element using my flashlight as a game host, that's more of an "open statement" inviting players to go check out something that might uniquely help them.

Sound

Having items react with "correct" or "incorrect" sounds helps players know that they are actively working with an interface. You can also have the interface announce progress by playing sounds louder and louder until they have completed their task. Game Masters can also activate certain sounds or even musical sequences to draw the attention of players.

Speech

Having characters explain something or tease the players for not knowing something is a great way to explain certain parts of the room to them without breaking the moment and just flat out providing a hint. Given the environment, teasing players about their lack of progress could be an especially strong language choice. "You coooould keep looking over there, but only if you never want to leave." There are standard lines delivered for every group. So much so, in fact, that you could have a professional actor record the lines and present them to the players in a specific character's voice.

Demonstration

Having a character mimic the action required by the players is a great way to introduce complicated concepts. You can use lenticular printing to demonstrate the motion by having the motions shown back and forth in the frames. These are also a great use for television screens in the rooms. Players could watch a security camera recording of the correct action and learn to mimic it.

Warning

Warnings are also one of the most common instructional elements that are naturally encountered in environments, especially dangerous environments where IPEs games are most likely to take place. Taking advantage of that, you can write warnings in the language of the game environment. You must be particularly careful to have the warnings clearly be fantasy warnings and not able to be mistaken for real warnings, however, as this may confuse the players. We use either noticeably antique warnings or warnings handwritten by the characters. "Solve it if you dare!" written in red paint is always a classic.

Labels

There can be many reasons why labels would exist in your environment. For example, if it was likely that hired help would be in and out of the area, there might be labels specifically letting them know where certain things are or how they might be used. The most common example would be to activate lighting. If a specific puzzle interface is a bit confusing contextually to players, then tying it to a lighting system should make its use clearer.

Blueprints

Blueprints, or basic construction plans, can be a great way to help players understand the dynamics of an environment. As game environments will typically be elaborate places (otherwise why would there be puzzles there?) it would make sense to have left-over blueprints. And, of course, a mastermind would certainly have prized blueprints of his works of genius explaining briefly how to use them for a patent office. There could even be blueprints highlighting weak spots in the system for future repairs.

Magnets

Sometimes it helps to use an actual physical force itself to guide players. If they need to put an object in just the right position for it to work or display a piece of information, then a magnet can help secure it. Otherwise, players might get frustrated at thinking they have the use of an object wrong and stop trying to place it into its correct position. A good time to use magnets as a clue is if you ever have a game master saying "make sure it's in the absolute correct position" to players. Players should always be rewarded when they put an object 90% into the right place and magnets can give them that last 10%. For example, we had a unique dial lock in our room that was a lot more fun for player when we incorporated magnets into the design so the correct dial "snapped" into place.

THE SECRETS OF GREAT PUZZLES

There are literally thousands of possible puzzles, but only a few that will truly shine in your room. So how do you find them? How do you get puzzles that can truly shine in your environment? The best answer is to choose the truly iconic. Icons evolved from focused religious expressions to anything that can be considered a strong representative symbol of something people find worthwhile. There are thousands of types of flowers, but our minds often rest on the icons of the rose, tulip, or orchid. Icons are objects people take easy, innate pleasure in seeing and set themselves apart from the general environment so much that they become the individual memories of an experience. Your environment is the entire panoramic shot full of color, form, and contrast, but the icon is the true focus of the picture and brings the meaning to the beauty. When I think about really great Escape Rooms I've played I'm easily able to remember specific puzzles that were unique to the room and perfect for the storyline. Bad puzzles fade way faster than the memories of certain artistic elements.

Picture searches online are great ways to discover the icon. Type in "beach scene" and you'll immediately see deck chairs and umbrellas, swinging palm trees and rippling waves, and deep blue skies over white beaches. This is the furniture, motion, and color that makes a beach scene iconic and a destination people dream about.

Type "amusement park scene" and you'll instantly see ferris wheels, bright lights, and a general sense of ordered chaos. Type "Cave Scene" and you'll see sloping rocks, a light peeking out of the cave, and calm, still waters on the cave floor. A lot of the work has been done for you visually: now it is up to you to incorporate these ideas more directly into puzzles.

A good shortcut for finding the iconic language for puzzles themselves is executive desk toys. Executive desk toys are fun, momentary distractions to the executive as well as an example of what defines the executive's personality to his guests. Similarly, a cool puzzle should be something with a cool personality just as much as it is something fun to play. It displays fascinating dynamics and mechanics as well as its beauty. It is something we want to not just see but understand. When is a puzzle great? When you can't help but touch it to see what it does next. Icons give us our sense of space and space well used. It is when a space feels dynamic that it truly feels engaging.

This section of the book is all about the search for greatness, so after each section there we be questions for you to ponder. Use this section wisely and it may be the best part of the book for expanding your puzzle development. Use it poorly and, well, I'd kinda love to see what you come up with anyway so have at it!

Showcase

One of the most common uses of an icon is the chance to "showcase" a particular value. The icon has been created to show something people consider a "classic." We see a complete product that is especially great at highlighting an important aspect. If we go to see a show case model car, then we might be looking at a highlighted interior space, reshaped exterior space, or the new power of the engine.

We also consider something "classic" when we know that it is the apex of the work. People aren't experimenting too much with sail boats these days so when we go and see one we know we are seeing the pinnacle of many years of hard work engineering the best possible physical product. Completed projects can be inherently interesting because we know the amount of effort it took to complete a project, from the initial spark of the idea to the many attempts and adjustments that went into the finished work ready for the public.

Showcase classic design

Sometimes a particular design creates a magical aura around it, like a rediscovered golden ratio. A lot of the greatest examples come from car designs. There are a few essential designs that span decades of functionality, but certain shapes of cars always hold people's interest, like the 1980's car of the, uh, future, the DeLorean. There is simply something about the car that gives people the chance to dream about power and the freedom of movement. But the DeLorean reminds us of the power of industrialization and the freedom of a future that only exists in Blade Runner movies. The particular boxy curves of the car, the emphasis on opening the doors as inconveniently as possible (note the loops they had to use to actually pull the door closed), the strange idea that squishing a car down makes it go faster. This design says so much and can easily be used to inspire a particular style in your puzzles.

Questions

Can the curves or the color of a puzzle be more evocative? Would the character who created the puzzle want to portray status through the puzzle's design? Would they have strange ideas of what a status is? Are there ways that the puzzle's speed or comfort can be enhanced? Can they be enhanced in ways that are "wrong" but still provocative? Can the design showcase a certain era's principles, such as independence, luxury, or economy?

Showcase classic function

A pirate ship invokes the imagination because it showcases many classic functions. As ships are made for the water, the display has an inherent buoyancy and idea of movement behind it. As it is made for piracy, the weapons and flags on display take on special meaning. A pirate ship is all you need to take on a hostile world and shape your own destiny. The Pirate ship also exposes the different roles of the crew because the sailors need to react immediately to the physical challenges of life on the sea. The watcher in the crow's nest, the men maintaining sails, the captain studying maps in his private quarters, each brings with it the contrast between high and low class; between military discipline and raucous freedom.

A ship becomes a display of an entire industry: you see how the wind is harnessed and the goods are stored. You understand where the pirates navigate and where they fight. It is all on a raw material display, the simplicity and immediacy of the transportation and its uses.

This display of function exists throughout many ancient works of man. Aqueducts transport water from the mountains to the city. A crackling firepit is the center of a blacksmith's forge. The harnessed power of steam allows the riverboat to glide to its destination. All of them have a clear display of function that especially intrigues modern people that are used to power being hidden away in cases of blinking electronic lights.

Questions

Are there ways to portray classic function in your puzzles? Is your room set in a time period when people had specific roles to maintain in the environment? Can you use ropes and pulleys? Look-outs and maps? Channels and nets? What special transportation or shipping tools exist in your environment? Can you reproduce factory functions? Cooking? Cleaning? Destruction? And, for futuristic or fantasy rooms, can you portray special modes of transportation that we dream about, such as teleportation or levitation? What are the expectations of basic function in your world?

Showcase classic high-volume design

People love the challenges of building that come specifically for high volume needs. A home kitchen is never as interesting as an industrial kitchen. When we are creating places that expect to hold large groups of people, the very shapes of the environment change. The ways we cook, the ways we sit, the ways we clean: there are mysterious dynamics involved when shifting the scale of comfort and pleasure to large accommodations. These dynamics come with unique possibilities for engagement and more specially trained roles. People especially enjoy working with volume tools because they maintain a lot of the same principles of home tools but are built with more power. We could never afford to pay for the extravagant lights and sounds of a rock concert with our own tickets, but when pooled together with others, we can share an amazing experience with a crowd of even thousands of other people. Giving your players access to a rock concert that casts them as the stars can fulfill a dream that otherwise will never come true. You can't give them the adoring fans, but you can give them the equipment that comes with the fame.

Questions

How can your environment portray functions built for the masses? Can the doors be larger? Can there be more seating than expected?

Are the tools available able to help a crowd of large people? What simple tool functions that your players already know can be amplified to have a large than life feel?

Showcase classic mechanics

As we were still learning to apply basic physics to machines, classic inventions would transparently portray the mechanics behind them. Catapults and pulleys clearly demonstrate the physical forces at work and so remain fun to experiment with as well as view in action. Watching mechanics in action gives players a chance to engage in classic puzzle principles like observation, experimentation, and lateral thinking. Working together to solve mechanical activities is one of the most ancient ways people worked together as a team to solve puzzles and gives your players chances to learn and excel in new roles as they conquer their challenges. While it can be difficult to use the full power of mechanical forces, mechanical illusions (such as seemingly heavy stones being catapulted across the room) can bring a lot of magic to a room's experience.

Questions

What mechanics can be displayed in your room? Can you use momentum, torque, or pressure in interesting ways? Are you able to use axles, pulleys, or inclined plane? Are their any mechanical illusions that would be wise to pursue?

Showcase classic sources of power

A large amount of power is always intriguing to people. Be it manmade, such as the power of industrial equipment, or the power of nature, like a waterfall or avalanche. Power brings special motion, lights, and sounds with it. Even just sorting through the aftermath of a powerful event can be exciting.

A lava lamp is a particularly great example of the hypnotic elements of power because it presents the illusion of power more than actual power. As the wax is heated by the light at the bottom of the lamp it slowly and smoothly floats up to cool off at the top of the lamp but the viewer is always reminded of the ancient power of lava and the destructive forces of energy. The powerful colors of red and yellow mix with the slow seamless motions of the wax to create the impression that much more powerful forces are at work. One of the greatest tricks of the lava lamp is that the power is not able to be directly inspected by the players, thus keeping the illusion intact. I know I was surprised when I first took off the lamp bottle and saw it was powered by a simple light bulb. But it is easy to keep players from overly inspecting your equipment and thus keep powerful illusion alive.

Questions

How can your puzzles use the idea and visuals of power? Can their colors shift to portray heat? Can the movement portray heavy motion? Can power be displayed in your room in ways players can see but not touch?

Showcase stacking materials

We are fascinated by how items fit together, whether it be a deck of cards or a ship full of containers. The ability to stack intrigues our sense of dimension and stability. In nature, we marvel the busyness of trees and the controlled chaos of a cloudy sky. On our desks, it's fun to stack magnetic objects to see how much we can bend the rules of gravity. The use of magnets increases this fascination, as the suspended materials almost become artistic. What should be just a group of metal beads becomes a perfectly structured pyramid that we would have to forcefully pry apart.

Questions

What items can be increased in your room? What can be multiplied? What can be squared away? What can be stacked together as an inaccessible display for the players, and what can be stacked together that players would enjoy interacting with? Are there any additional forces you can add to the objects you stack, such as an organizational method, or tools that can further the player's stacking ability?

Showcase the internal

Complex machines and buildings need to be protected and supported from the weather and unskilled hand, so all have casings built around them to protect and hide them. Yet we all love the chance to take a peak into the electric box or see a god's eye view of a building's interior design. We love to view the interior of a machine because it exposes the carefully crafted engineering that solved the problems of space, material, and design, and efficiency to give us a refined product. The symphony of the various parts gets closer the more we see it dangerously exposed. The more you put layers in charge of exposing secrets the more powerful they will feel.

Questions

What inner workings can you display in your room? Are there access panels players can open to solve a puzzle inside? Can they view the backstage process of a company? Are there ways that they can feel as if they are seeing forbidden or fantastic sights?

Emphasis

When we go to see works of art we love to see how artists emphasize their subjects. The human drama of a moment, the holy high of religious expression, the shocking low of violence actions, the beauty of a landscape and the mystery of an abstraction all come together to drive unique expressions that we couldn't run across in any other circumstance. The endless worlds we can gaze into tell us of the dreams and nightmares of the author and the parts of their souls they want to express with us.

Similarly, puzzles can bring moments of emphasis that help us appreciate just how special our experience is. Anything can be highlighted in a puzzle but in professional design its usually best to come up with highlights that also simplify the puzzle process. People want to be able to understand the puzzles they are working on fairly quickly and so emphasis helps us have less working pieces and clearer concepts.

Emphasize the tone

Often on executive desktops, horror, fantasy, cute, or "punk" elements will be captured in objects that would otherwise be utilitarian. A regular clock can become a Lovecraftian horror when the struggle between a diver and the dark tentacles of the sea are enshrined in twisted brass that encircles the normal clock. A desk without any emotional elements seems bare. I myself have a forky on my desk from Disney's Toy story to remind me of the optimism that comes from viewing the world differently.

We especially love to evoke the visuals of our childhoods: the memories of time spent on worlds that were created just to spark our imagination. There are a lot of ways to increase our sense of place and style, and every puzzle should make use of established toy themes as often as possible.

Questions

What are the strong elements of tone in your world that enable players to bring their history of imagination to the experience? Can things be cuter? Scarier? Are there ways to make the theme of the room come even more alive, even if they push the boundaries of the realistic?

Emphasize the physics

Toy components can make the use of physics themselves as an art form. There are many magical capabilities in physics: projection, spinning, and forces of energy. Because we rarely get a chance to play with gratuitous physics, it makes perfect sense to use them in the puzzle world and explore their capabilities in full. We love the chance to spin, to lift, and to fling objects to their destinations.

Questions

What physical moments in the room can be made greater? What parts of the game world can be given more elements of expression simply because they show us motion, rotation, levers, or other mechanics we rarely get to see in the day to day?

Handle

To be able to handle something strange or interesting is one of our most primary expressions of curiosity. Often we do not truly know something until we can feel it in our hands. There are different physical sensations associated with fragile or durable objects. Objects that are cold to the touch feel clinical while objects warm to the touch feel alive. There are characteristics of items that immediately invite play, when they are soft, slimy, or responsive.

Handle Magnets

People love playing with magnetic forces. The sudden snap of connection and feel of a mysterious pull are of great use in puzzles. Besides being a great source for surprising lock mechanisms, magnets can also help people solve puzzles by making physical connections clearer or highlighting certain clues. They're also great at moving objects through walls or over floors. Taking as much advantage of magnets in gameplay as possible is always a good choice and they lend themselves especially well to sci-fi or fantasy themes. Magnets are already a well know staple of IPEs but their usage, when done well, is an evergreen highlight of the experience.

Questions

What sudden connections of force could be added to your puzzles? Can you use magnets to provide unique clues to the players? Can magnets be used to create a more unique puzzle interface? Can they be used in any locks or with any tool puzzles?

Handle Fluids

The special manipulation of fluids has a hypnotic appeal to people. The flow and control of water, both out in the open and inside pipes, has fascinating motions and, given the addition that it is difficult to control, immediately impresses players by the special preparation and maintenance the game has put into its show. I was once astounded by being given the freedom to pour water into a pot to retrieve a key that was floating inside. Even a puzzle as simple as pouring in the context of an IPE can be spell binding for players.

Questions

What way can fluids be used in your room? Can the illusion of fluid be used? Is your setting specifically associated with water? Can fluid be used as part of an environmental element?

Handle Dominos

Dominos are the best possible display of the delicate nature of order. They provide the ability to collapse an entire fragile system and see the consequences of that collapse. There is also a special power in the acknowledgement of how difficult the set-up of dominos must be for the staff and it's true, more than half the challenge with using dominos in design is figuring out how to set them up again easily, just like how we are fascinated with the racking of bowling pins.

Questions

Is there anything in your room that can be set-up to be knocked down? Is there anything in your room that can start a surprising chain reaction? Are there ways to display pieces so that players will be impressed by the amount of time and energy that has gone into your game's setup?

Handle Marbles

It's always exciting to have objects come alive with motion and face challenges in their own special ways and the best object by far for this task is the workhorse of the marble. It's just the perfect vehicle for stunt travel is the marble: the reflective sphere that easily glides through unique stunts such as spinning wheels, dropping levels, and rotating funnels. One of my prized positions is the arcade size pinball machine that resides in my living room. Setting up marble mazes and tracks is also an easier reset for game masters as they only need to reset the beginning position of the marble and the first position of the marble controls.

Questions

What motion in your room could be accentuated with marbles? Could marbles release as part of a puzzle? Could you use marbles for a maze or tool puzzle in your room? Could marbles be used as the controls of a puzzle?

Handle Unique materials

There are a lot of fun materials that are possible to play with in rooms. Gooey materials and other objects people would want to manipulate and touch. Playing with slime and other unique textures give players the "gross" factor that can be especially fun to experience. Feathers and silks are great if your room can have a lot of clothes or luxury elements. Even stone can be intriguing in the right contexts: whatever materials that are especially unique in your game environment should be incorporated into your gameplay as much as possible.

Questions

Are you able to use unique substances in your room? Are you able to add weird textures to puzzles and experiences? Can you make something surprising soft or stretchy? Are their food, building, furniture, or clothing elements that can add unique materials to your particular environment?

Alter

One of the final ways to add interesting points to your puzzle room is to take what is expected and alter it in a surprising manner. People love to have their expectations played with while experiencing a game. It provides the right level of novelty without feeling foreign or strange. Clever alterations can be some of the best ways to reward lateral thinking among your players.

Alter the expected

A lot of objects are iconic for their actions, and these recognizable designs can be given new physical roles in IPE gameplay. For example, we are always used to striking a bell to make noise, but a bell can just as easily become a bucket for carrying water if the need arises.

You can alter the expected attitudes of characters the players encounter. A medieval knight is expected to be pompous and look down on the player's actions. If, instead, the knight does honor to the players and hands them the one true sword to fight the dragon, then the importance of the players is noticeably increased by the altered outcome.

Questions

What are defined roles in your world that could be played with? Could a hero become an ally, or a villain a friend? What are uses of tools, decorations, or buildings that can be changed in surprising ways? What can be given unique life by changing how it usually works to fit a new need? Can any of your chosen puzzles use expected puzzle dynamics in surprising ways?

Alter the efficient

Making functions as straightforward as possible is a necessary way of life because we can't have gratuitous parts or processes slowing us down. If something is expected to be used daily or quickly it can't have flashy extra features that make it more difficult to use. But puzzles are allowed to have spinning pieces, random lights, and gratuitous moments. A marble can spin around a flashing basin before entering a hole. A computer can flash random pictures before executing a command. The lights can go out before the door opens. While as a general rule you never want these dramatic flashes to last more than few seconds, the ability to add dramatic moments to your room needs to be thoroughly explored. I recommend writing a list of effects possible for your world and then going through your puzzles to see where they might be easily added.

Questions

What fun gratuitous functions can be added to your puzzles? What mechanical or electric effects would be fun to see? What mechanics can be lengthened or even shortened to make their usage surprising?

Alter the complexity

Games that normally have many pieces can be reduced to be simpler to play, or games that are normally simple can be made more difficult. For example, a checkers game can have the general size of the board reduced so the game play is much faster. Or a game of tic tac toe could be played on multiple boards at the same time. The more familiar your group is with general puzzle types the more they'll enjoy seeing the game altered in a fantastic way. One of the greatest selling points of an IPE game is that they give us games that are larger than life and can never comfortably fit in the living room. They are truly destination experiences.

Questions

What classic games can be made simpler in your room? What easy games can be made more complex but still retain the rules of game play that the players already know? Are their pieces of other puzzle types that can be ramped up or down in their complexity in surprising ways?

Alter the size

There is a lot of amusement when it comes to playing a game with familiar rules on a unfamiliar scale. Executives will often shrink games to play them on their desk. A game of tic tac toe can be played with bean bags so, while the mechanics are still simple, the sheer effort of play makes up for the simplicity of the game. A game of chess can be played with huge three-foot-tall pieces. Or a game of football can be shrunk down and played on a table. What could have once required a whole team of people can now be accomplished by one person, or on the other hand, a chess game that once required one person could now require an entire team moving the pieces.

Questions

What can be shrunk or expanded in ways that will be fun for players to interact with? What would be surprising to become large and clunky, or amusing to become intricate and modern?

Alter the time period

"Punk" styles are taking elements of one time period and applying them to another. The past can be made more technologically complex with robots serving roman senators. And the future can be full of inefficient devices with steam powering computers. But, best of all, the future can be faked. The elaborate inventions we dream of can be secretly controlled by the game master behind the scenes, making the technical performance much more forgiving. By messing with how the technological time period works in the room you are creating environments where random puzzles are much more expected. A roman palace with futuristic devices would "naturally" have more modern locks than the actual time period. Never be afraid to have a "great inventor" creating astounding marvels in your time period.

Questions

Can your room accommodate a fantasy of the past or future? Can you place time period elements into your room? Would your characters be particularly enamored with a period of time and so introduce time period elements into your room "in character"?

In-world Puzzle Profile

Every puzzle needs an in-world puzzle profile in order to confirm it properly fits in the game's reality. While there are a lot of great puzzles, not all of them will meet the parameters of a game's reality. For example, a pulley rope puzzle, while being exciting in a pirate adventure, would seem strange in a sci-fi setting. And yet sometimes a puzzle design may just be so cool that you might want to know the right ways to bend the room's reality to accommodate it. The puzzle profile will help you place the puzzle in the most dynamic way for the game's environment.

A puzzle profile is made up of the five essential questions: "Why?" "Who?" "What" "How" and "When?" All of a puzzle's story and physical parameters can be broken into these five categories and ensure a complete experience.

Why?

The most important part of your puzzle's profile is going to be the "why." Are the puzzles there to protect a secret, guard a treasure, test a skill, entertain a guest, or create a scientific miracle? Do they supply a resource such as power or information? The "why" of your puzzle is the heart of your story because it channels the power and purpose of the puzzle. If the puzzle seems extraneous or is just an obstacle for the sake of having an obstacle, then the players won't feel engaged in your environment and, more importantly, won't feel they are affecting or changing it. A sense of story progression without being bogged down by story explanations provides the most excitement to players and a well thought out "why" to the purpose of puzzles is the best way to provide it.

One of my puzzle room designs was to create a "Santa Puzzle Room." Unfortunately, there wasn't a good sense of "why" in any of the puzzles. Santa's Village is supposed to be open to everyone so it didn't make sense that people would need to solve puzzles to open doors or turn on Santa's machines. To cover this I invented a character, Noel, the angry elf who thought no one had the spirit of Christmas so he locked up all of Santa's warehouse. Players had to solve puzzles to prove they had the Christmas spirit. But inviting such a strange concept meant I had to struggle against media apathy for the entire game. In the final room you were supposed to create the perfect toy for Noel by using Santa's toy making machines and Noel's secret designs.

By making his favorite toy you restored his faith in Christmas. But every group struggled with this story line and spent the time desperately pressing every flipped switch until at last a toy popped out of the machine. My "why" was a spectacular failure. It wasn't an organic experience and, even though some people enjoyed the puzzles themselves, no one enjoyed the story and, in fact the story became one of the chief obstacles of the room.

Who?

The second most important part is the "who" as a puzzle designed with a good "who" in mind brings the character's stories to life. Strong characters are the ones who make larger-than-life decisions and this fits well into the world of puzzle games. Using puzzles to protect your treasure begs eccentric characters and odd motivations.

In my haunted theater design, there are two main characters: the beautiful, vain actress Rose and her brilliant, eccentric husband Henry who jealously guards her at his theater. He designs strange contraptions that run the theater with unique controls for the lighting, sound, and music. His strange designs demonstrate a brilliant but complicated mind, and that mind surely could snap if he is betrayed. One night he discovers that Rose is planning to leave him and she vanishes completely, never to be seen again. Now it is up to the players to use Henry's devices and discover what happened to her those many years ago.

"Who" can also be answered by a group of people. In a temple of doom game I designed, the temple puzzles are designed by the temple guards who we never meet but make their presence known by designing traps that challenge any who would try to take their idol's eye. As they were designed as a group with a united purpose, the puzzles are more defined by their general mythology than any personal motivation but they still have a huge presence in the game.

What?

"What" is the physical composition of the puzzle itself. The main part of "what" is the materials chosen for the puzzle. Did the characters use common or unique materials to construct the puzzle? What type of materials would most likely exist in the environment and what materials would seem outlandish?

One of the most important parts of "what" is to minimize follow-up questions. It can already be difficult to explain every question you could ask in a room filled with strange puzzles, so the more minimal the curiosities the better. A mad inventor would probably design a puzzle with extraneous parts, and he would certainly have metal pieces lying around his laboratory, so it would make sense that the puzzle would be made of metal. A temple guard would design a puzzle to test the "worthiness" of a player with a permanent, imposing interface so it would make sense for him to use the available stone in the temple. A top tech security guard would have a touch screen technology interface that you could "hack" because that's the most likely interface for day-to-day tech work. But would a sci-fi captain use wood to create a maze to turn on the ship's engine? Where would a spaceship get the extra wood, and why would a maze be crafted from it? In that case, the follow-up "whys" to the "what" start to bog down the game.

Sometimes the "what" idea in your head is too good to be ignored, however, and a puzzle needs to exist because it's too awesome to pass. That reason itself can be enough because your players will appreciate the awesomeness. The captain could have believed that his wood maze was so cool he had to carry it to space with him. "Because it is awesome" becomes the official "in-story" explanation. After all, when we visit a friend's home and see an oversized toy we don't question but know they have it because they love the toy. All puzzle environments can justify having "toys" in them. Seeing a pinball in a Colonial period home makes sense if the owner really loves pinball.

How?

"How" is a more subtle question but can lend greater depth to your room. How was the puzzle constructed? Did they use unique tools? Were they skilled or amateur workers? Did they use real world physics or fantasy physics to construct their device?

Just like in the movie "Roger Rabbit," players can adapt to rules that are stretched or even opposite of the real world as long as those rules are consistently applied. Roger Rabbit can do anything "as long as it's funny" and players can accept time and space being bent "as long as it solves puzzles." If the physics need to be "bent" for one puzzle to properly work, then there might be ways to use that same bent physics throughout the room to create a more consistent experience. For example, if some bricks are light weight, all bricks can be light weight with the explanation that the players are just that super strong.

When?

"When" is the least important aspect, but the consideration of it can help you better present your character's backstory and the history of the room. Was the puzzle created during an optimistic or pessimistic time in the character's life? In the heyday of the environment or during its decay? Most of the backstory would be frustrating to outright let players know, but the layering of time when subtlety presented can be an intriguing wrinkle in the room.

Final Puzzle selection Factors

Now that you've found your most iconic designs and grounded them in the reality of your game it's time for the hardest part: making the final cut. Luckily, three final factors should help you make the best decision.

Realism

How true to reality would it be to have your puzzle be part of the environment? How long is your puzzle profile and how much did you have to stretch the truth to make it fit? Remember that shorter stories are not just better but feel truer to the players. So what is truly most likely to be created by the characters? What sounds the most natural and what sounds the most strained?

Movie Expectations

Return to the beginning of why you chose this particular puzzle room: what are the movie expectations of the game? What puzzles have developed to fit those moments best? Return to the movies and video games that first inspired you and think about where you would place your puzzles in the media. What experiences feel most essential? What puzzles did you create that should have been in the movie? Your game should ultimately be a more exciting experience than the movie, so have you succeeded?

Fun

When it all gets down to it: what's the most fun? What would you be most excited to share with friends or play yourself? What's something you've always wanted to see or do in a room but haven't had the chance to do yet? When you're down to the last few puzzles to cut and you have to go with your head or your heart trust your heart. After all, you're going to see people playing this puzzle over and over again. It's better if it's one you enjoy yourself.

Puzzle Checklist

Keep these principles in mind while you go over your puzzles with a final check list. You don't have to answer every question, but this list is a good summary of all the ideas and principles that I've listed throughout these chapters.

Do your players have to have any pre-existing knowledge or skills before starting the puzzle (understanding how riddles work, how to interact with pieces, how a tool works, etc.)

Are there multiple approaches to solving the puzzle that players can take? (Just moving things around until it works, bending pieces into place, guessing at the word)

Does the environment fit the puzzle and react to the puzzle?

Are the rules and goal of the puzzle as clearly defined as possible?

Is the core mechanic of the puzzle clearly defined?

Can the core mechanic of the puzzle benefit from a challenge curve?

What are the portions of skill, time, luck, and thought in solving the puzzle?

Can multiple success states be added for overcoming the challenge?

Will the final success have a single guaranteed result?

Will the final success state be permanent?

How likely are players to have encountered the puzzle or elements of the puzzle before?

What does failing the puzzle look like? Does it require a reset by the player?

How will advanced players tackle the puzzle?

SHINING A LIGHT ON THE WHOLE GAME

Game Experience Verb

The active verb of the game defines the entire experience. Discover. Escape. Defend. Explore. The main verb is evocative of time spent in a land of threatening or intriguing landscapes. These breathe life into the epic journeys that all children dream of undertaking, or the startling adventures mankind is yet to imagine. The verb can even change as the players learn more and interact in the environment, as long as each change is clearly directed to the players.

The verb "Discover" is a great opening to a sci-fi game, but as the players learn about innocent alien life on the planet and the evil overlords that want to destroy it the game can shift to "defend" and then as the players get more confident about saving the galaxy can shift again to "attack." Each switch in the verb has different actions expected by players to do and new activities to learn. The players discover the alien life and learn its ways, then they learn how to defend the alien life, and finally they learn how to attack the evil forces and stop the universe overlords for all time.

The final verb of the game can even be a surprise. In the haunted theater game, the players don't start exploring the space with the idea they'll soon become the theater's final actors. But as they learn about the history of the theater they discover that is the only way to set the diva's spirit free. The verb "search" is replaced by "perform" and so the stakes are raised higher for the players.

One important principle is that as the verb shifts in the game it must always increase in intensity. If players feel that their story has reached a natural climax but it keeps going it can be hard to recapture energy. If the Sci-fi game had one more verb after "attack" the game would probably be less satisfying. If the attack left the players stranded on the planet and they then had to solve another series of puzzles to "return" to the ordinary world, then the game's storyline starts to become tedious. In life, all fun activities have a "return to normal" moment. You head back from the beach, clean up after a meal, shower after a work-out. Removing the ordinary "return" verb for the players is one of the highlights of the experience you're offering.

However, if you need a denouement (or wrap-up) period for the game for the storyline to be complete, then some simply pressing of buttons is a great way to give your players a victory lap. If, after defeating the aliens, all they have to do is press a button to send the ship back to Earth then you're rewarding them for becoming the masters of their environment. By knowing immediately what to do it isn't one last puzzle and, by having what they need to do be incredibly easy, it doesn't become a chore. The focus, like in any good story, must be on making the denouement period as short as possible.

Doors

The best way to mark the different acts is with doors. Doors gather all the players into one spot and have them all focus on moving forward, so they are excellent moments to advance the story or change the threat level. However, it is not always necessary to have a physical door. Doors are the bottleneck moments of the game, when all the available options and puzzles have narrowed to one point and a door must be opened to make additional progress. While most commonly a physical door, it can also be equipment turning on, the weather changing, or a new threat appearing. This moment can be used to alter the dynamics of the story because everyone will be paying attention to one fixed point and not individually focused on solving puzzles or searching for clues.

However, once the door is opened another important dynamic must be considered: are players able to backtrack through it to previous points in the game? This gives us the three general classifications of doors: "pull" for doors the players control, "push" for doors the game master controls, and "swinging" for doors in which control is shared between the player and the game master.

Pull Doors

Pull doors are the most common. When the door is unlocked by the players, they step it into a completely new situation filled with new challenges. The change is activated by the players and under their control, so the players can choose if they like to step back through the door and return to their old setting. There could be unfinished puzzles in the previous room or some players might want to enjoy the scenery at their leisure. However, it is usually less fun to have players backtrack to previous rooms because it robs the story of a sense of progression and keeps the players from feeling that they have "leveled up" or advanced as heroes. A new room gives the players a chance to feel the stakes have been raised or they are in a new environment where the skills they have learned so far will be put to greater tests. Backtracking to previous rooms is rarely the most fun path for players and should be minimized.

Variations

The pull door may be hidden in the environment. For example, players could know they need to be looking for a secret tunnel in the room but would never expect that casting a magic spell will cause the book case to swing open and reveal a new passage. The concrete action of a move initiated and controlled by the players remains the same.

Players can also have a "gate" situation in which they can see through the door to the next environment but they are not able to go through it until they solve enough challenges. This can cause more excitement as there can be a build-up for entering the new place.

The environment can also change around them due to their actions, creating a new situation that acts like entering a new room. For example, trying to cure zombies can bring on a zombie attack. The players spend the first part of the game manufacturing a cure. The players know that to test their cure they will need to start fighting the zombie horde so when they are ready they make the choice to let the zombies in. Whether or not their cure works, the players have made the decision to move the game forward and alter their environment. The consequences of that action, such as zombies knocking open shelves to reveal shotguns for an arcade puzzle, flow from the actions the players clearly took themselves.

Push Doors

A push door is much rarer in rooms because players stumble forward but are not allowed to go back. Either they can never return to the previous room or they must find a way to unlock the push doors in order to return.

Push doors can be especially exciting, however, because they make outside forces more noticeable and give the players less control of their universe while still clearly being the heroes.

Variations

Push doors can easily be translated into other game actions, such as activating a portal to a new location or sliding down into a dark room without easily being able to return. Players do make a choice in these scenarios, either pushing a button or leaping onto a slide, but they do not know the consequences of their actions and there are no clear warnings on what will happen next. Players can even be pushed through these doors at certain designated times of the story. For instance, in a haunted house game, the angry spirits can return at the half-way mark of the game, no matter how many puzzles the players have yet to solve.

In the zombie attack scenario, the players can be manufacturing a cure until a surprise zombie attack. The computer equipment they were using breaks and the players have no choice but to fight the zombies. Attempting to cure them is no longer an option in the game and the tension will shift to escaping the lab after the attack is complete. Players can possibly find a way to repair the computer, but they will have to work extra hard to accomplish that goal and still achieve the "cure" ending.

Swinging doors

Finally, there are swinging doors between two different environments in which players are able to move freely back and forth. Swinging doors are great for rooms in which the layout presents a clear series of challenges, but the challenges might be paced to appear back and forth in each area or require resources to be prepared in one area and then used in another. The areas are clearly distinct in their usages, but the story can overlap between them and even happen simultaneously in them. For example, in a game in which there is a kitchen area and a dining area, the chef can announce that the restaurant is now serving the dessert course in the kitchen and, simultaneously, the dessert menu can appear to the customers in the dining area. It is still up to the players to make and serve the desserts in the separate areas.

Variations

The doors to the environment represent a clear shift in how the environment is being used. In the restaurant example, there are clear shifts between creating and serving food. There can also be ebb and flow situations in which players must switch between spending money and earning. The area can also switch between day and night and have unique challenges for surviving each, such as in "Minecraft."

In the zombie example, a swinging door environment has the players go back and forth between testing cures and fighting zombies. Players will know they have to take breaks from testing when the zombie forces get so overwhelming that they shut down the power, but once the zombies have been fought back, players are able to turn the power back on and keep searching for the cure. The back and forth will eventually end in either the zombies winning and taking over the laboratory or successfully being cured.

Classic Ride Layouts

Theme Park rides have several classical layouts that help their guests get the most out of the ride. These layouts can be used to plan the physical progress of solving your puzzles and review the optimal flow of your game. By adjusting the flow to better fit a ride layout you create a smoother and more exciting game experience. The best part is that a lot of these ride layouts, while currently existing in theme parks, are still mostly theoretical IPEs. If you want to really experiment with your game then this is the section for you!

Classic Loop

The classic loop is the simplest presentation that leads players from one moment to the next without any overlap. It is one clean loop through the entire experience. Like the dark ride, "it's a small world," players drift forward from scene to scene and, while the loop can still build to a climactic final scene using elements the players have seen before, there is still no overlap in the ride layout, so the final scene is entirely new objects even if they do repeat previously seen themes.

A loop layout is great for IPE games that will have a lot of rooms or are more geared for first time players. By having players smoothly progress through the room they can be assured they are seeing everything and can be confident in their progress.

Pulled loop

The pulled loop keeps a lot of the pacing of the classic loop but bends inwards towards a specific environment or theme, weaving in and out of a place while still progressing forward. The loop ends up looking more like a flower head. The Matterhorn bob sled in Disney World uses this model, as you dart in and out of the mountain while always sliding down. Sometimes, the ride can circle around a certain action, like Splash Mountain that continues to come back to and build upon the impending rush of the final climactic drop.

The pulled loop is great for rooms in which players will keep coming back to a central theme, like piloting a spaceship, building a robot, or defeating a monster. The more that they explore and return to the center, the greater they will feel they are chipping away at an impossible task worthy of their time and attention.

Spaghetti

The spaghetti structure exists when the loop starts to bend on itself so much that the progression of the ride becomes harder to trace. Basically, the ride progression looks like a mess of spaghetti thrown on the floor: sure it's still all one loop, but it is a messy, squishy loop. Like the classic dark ride, "Peter Pan" in Disney world, we start to see the world from different angles and weave in and out of every nook and cranny.

The spaghetti layout is about getting the most of your environment and seeing it from every angle. While it is not as smooth as the classic loop or a centered as the pulled loop, it is important that a clear progression is still being made and that players never double back onto the same position. Puzzle elements can bunch together but once complete, a puzzle is never returned to or reactivated. For example, once you solve a puzzle it may flip around and reveal a new puzzle on the opposite side of the wall: but you are still solving a new puzzle. This is great for a room that has a "behind-the-scenes" element to it, like a carnival, fun house, or restaurant. You wouldn't be surprised to see both sides of a mirror when exploring a fun house but you never have to return to a previous room.

The Race Track

The racetrack is used when a thrilling and fast paced part of the ride is the most important part, like on the Disney rides "Fast Track" or "Radiator Springs Racers." While some of the ride is built in a loop fashion to set up the game, most of the ride uses one exciting moment to define the experience. In a puzzle room, it would be one great activity dominating the experience.

This is great for rooms with focuses on great events, like putting on a play or retrieving an item from the temple of doom. It could also be used if your room ended with a large battle, either in space against a monster or against a final army of zombies. A lot of the play components need to be plugged into the final moment that will win the game.

There and back

The "there and back" layout is used for arcade rides in which guests can shoot at targets several times throughout the course of the game. It gives several different regrouping moments in between the moments of larger activity. Think of it as a sling shot model. Players are pushed in front of the activity, give it their all, then bounce back again to reload or catch a breather. The best example of this ride type is the "Toy Story" arcade game where you move back and forth between various displays wracking up points with your gun.

This is great for games that have battle sections as players can battle before looping back and preparing for another challenge. This is best for groups of villains that the players can expect to battle in a variety of environments like zombies, space aliens, or a serial killer. This is also a good model for competition rooms. And, at least at the moment, it's a pretty experimental new model. You might be the first to launch it!

Mirror Layout

A layout where a prominent amount of the game doubles back on previous track from a new perspective. This has been used in reverse roller coasters or on trackless dark rides. Doubling back and seeing previous parts of the ride also usually gives riders the chance to see other riders or ride "secrets" as they progress.

This is used in games where one great reversal where players backtrack to use the same series of puzzles before exiting a room, such as switching back to a previous time or going through an "upside down" version of the game. This would also make sense if players had to backtrack and redecorate a portion of the room, either to make it right for a celebration or to set up a trap for a villain. There are a lot of exciting possibilities and I've heard tales of rooms that have used this layout though I've yet to play them myself.

Twisted Spaghetti

And here we are, the most difficult and, at this point, almost entirely theoretical ride layout. This is a spaghetti layout that actually does double back on to previous sections of track in order to complete the run. This is the most complicated and most trackless rides available like "Star Wars: Rise of the Resistance" which, at least when I published this book, is one of the hardest theme park rides to get to in the world.

This could have mirror elements, race track elements, there and back elements. It could be a classic loop that turns and goes completely in reverse. This is basically whatever you'd like it to be with only one rule: the track does indeed twist on itself.

Which, in a puzzle room scenario, means returning to puzzles that were previously thought completed. The puzzles players return to would have "leveled up" with additional components and materials they have gathered from other experiences and now need to use again. This could be used in a haunted mansion setting where you learn more about the characters and gain more equipment during your journey. By returning to old rooms with new equipment you can uncover even greater secrets that will help you purify the house. I also thought I could have used this to great effect in my Santa game: returning to previous portions of the game to decorate it for Christmas and make it more magical. But, unfortunately, Santa's in storage so I don't have a chance to try at the moment. So you'll have your own chance to make a Christmas wish come true!

Intensity Structures

Intensity structures come in three acts, with each act having a different level of engagement. IPE rooms cannot accommodate complicated narratives, so the lowering and raising of intensity become the main story progression for the players. Intensity structures don't depend on the heightened stakes of a straightforward narrative (such as the players getting in increasing danger as the story progresses), but instead the heightened stakes of visual and emotional intensity. This is the part of the story that has the greatest visuals or is the most exciting for the audience when they truly don't know what will happen next. For example, in the "Wizard of Oz" the greatest shift in intensity happens early in the film from when the world changes from black and white to vivid color. While Dorothy still has no idea what real challenges will face her in the world of Oz, the visually heightened scene of stepping into the Munchkin village is the most intense portion of the film. The third act, when she knows to fight the witch, isn't as intense as this moment, even though all she is doing is stepping into a peaceful village. We also get a sense when she steps into the village that she is no longer restricted by her Kansas lifestyle but can in fact do anything or be anyone. She is given powers and possibilities that expand her world and are most exciting when she doesn't quite know what to do with them yet. When the visuals and constrictions are ramping up or slowing down, players can sense the change and appreciate that the narrative is progressing.

Intensity structures follow the rule of three in stories: that something must change three times for the audience to really feel they understand it. A complete journey has a beginning, middle, and end. Players, since they are living that journey, need a clear sense of the progression and the shifts in intensity help them mark their journeys.

One of the easiest ways to test the intensity of a particular act is how easily you remember the key visuals of that act. Since threats can come in all shapes and sizes, it is the power of the visual that best defines the moment. The Bond villain is not just another thug for Bond to dispatch in the middle of the story, but with his eye patch, pet cat, and tank full of sharks, battling him obviously becomes the most intense moment in the film from the unique visuals alone.

1-2-3 Intensity Structure – Battle an enemy

A 1-2-3 intensity structure is an "increasing challenge." It grows with breaks and twists in the tension until it is finally defeated. A classic example is "Indiana Jones and the Raiders of the Lost Ark." While battling in different exotic locations, the clear threat of the Nazis and their desire to collect magical artifacts grows stronger throughout the film. The tricks, techniques, and knowledge Indiana Jones must use to defeat them grow along with the threat.

For memorable visuals, In Indiana Jones, there is the beginning temple with the rolling of stones, the use of the staff of Ra in the "well of souls" and the complete destruction of the Nazis when they open the ark and literally melt before its power. Each scene's visual clearly builds on the last with more at stake and greater threats of destruction.

A three-act structure can also be entirely about defeating a single obstacle. Whether a giant monster, an entire army, or even an arduous journey. Godzilla as a monster grows as a threat. The characters don't just attack the monster several times but each time they learn more about how to proceed and regroup to try new tactics. Battling an army starts with scouts discovering their position, continues with an initial skirmish, then finishes with a huge fight to the death. An arduous journey starts out with supplies, then has the supplies run out, and then has the hero struggle to maintain their spirit against all odds until the journey is complete. Each of these threats builds up and uses several different mental and physical resources to be defeated.

1-3-2 Intensity Structure – Surprise threat

A 1-3-2 intensity structure has a subdued first act that introduces the concepts and tension, but then the threat presents itself as strong and overwhelming before a third act in which the threat is defeated following usual means. This will be typically a story where a sudden reveal of the true nature of the threat comes with strong visuals that are most vivid but once the heroes overcome the shock of the true nature of the threat they are able to defeat it using fairly conventional means.

In "The Texas Chainsaw Massacre," the murder of the heroine's friends sets a frightening pace for the film, but when Sally thinks she has escaped to the gas station, the revelation that the gas station attendant is part of the same evil family is the strongest shock of the film, with Sally's subsequent final escape follows more standard beats. She is simply able to finally flee, free of the delusions she will get local help. The insane family is the most vibrant, novel part of the story as Sally learns just how evil they are. The climax of the escape, while still full of tension, is more of a downhill experience because the escape is an inevitable moment led by the audience expectation. It would be too depressing for Sally to die at the end of the film, so it's never a realistic expectation in the mind of the audience. The horror of the family, then, is what sticks most in your mind. A video game that follows this structure is "Resident Evil 7" where fighting the family in the middle of the game is more exciting than fighting the inevitable generic villain at the end.

3-1-2 Intensity Structure – Discover a new world

A "3-1-2 intensity structure" is great for stories that transport the characters into entirely new worlds and thus the shock of adjusting to the world has the story at its most intense. While the story can then build into a climax at the end, nothing is greater than the shock of being transported someplace new at the beginning of the story.

To return to the example of the "Wizard of Oz," the tornado and introduction of Oz are the strongest moments of the film. Dorothy gathering her friends becomes a less compelling middle sequence, and the battle of the witch and escaping of Oz, while higher points in the story, do not have the same visual tension of the beginning of the film.

3-2-1 Intensity Structure – Battle a world

The 3-2-1 is an environmental disaster intensity structure. In the "Poseidon Adventure," it is the action of the ballroom being turned upside down that is the most memorable and intense moment. The fallout of the story is the group gathering together and being rescued. The closer they get to being rescued, the less intense the movie feels. The same is true for the movie "Independence Day." While the battle at the end of the movie is interesting, the most intense moment is when the aliens reveal themselves and destroy so many national monuments. Turning the world upside down because of a disaster is more engaging than watching people fight to restore it.

The 3-2-1 structure is also the most common Escape Room structure. When you are locked in a prison, you start with the challenge at its chief point: limited options and control. As you progress and gain more and more control of your environment the threat is lessened. Especially as the group learns the "language" of the room and becomes more confident in tackling its challenges.

2-1-3 Intensity Structure – Surprise new enemy

The "2-1-3" intensity structure is more rare, as it separates the two most shocking elements of the film with a middle that has a simmering threat to connect the two most intense points. It is often used to introduce a "surprise new enemies," when a character is thrown into a war but manages to fight back the enemy and then focus on strengthening his position. Once prepared, he has a spectacular final battle.

"Home Alone" has this structure, with Kevin struggling to overcome the "surprise enemy" of being alone in the first Act but then fighting alone against the thieves in the contraption-ridden Act 3. The initial fun of the movie is his being home alone and learning how to survive on his own with a very small Act 2 when he starts to change his focus towards fighting the villains and tricking them into thinking his house is full. As he learns more about them and becomes more responsible for protecting his home. It is in Act 3 that the movie shines brightest.

The visuals support this. The screams of the mother and son in the beginning are more remembered than the middle section of the film in which he tricks the burglars by making it seem like he is having a Christmas party at his house. But nothing is better than the crazy contraptions in the finale of the film.

2-3-1 Intensity Structure – Surprise new World

A "2-3-1 intensity structure" is used in "end of the world" stories to present the surprise of what the new world will be. The shock of the world ending starts intense and becomes more intense before finally taking a more subdued tone at the end of the story. Zombie movies are the most common examples. In "Shawn of the Dead" the initial shock of zombies and gathering the party together to get to the bar is intense and transitions into the final fight at the bar. But the army retaking London from the zombies happens almost entirely off screen and the post-apocalyptic world just accepts having zombie best friends as day-to-day living.

The Titanic uses the threat of social tension in the first act to set the stage for the destruction of the Titanic in the 2nd Act. The third

Act of Rose surviving in the waters of the wreckage of the Titanic, is a final wrap-up tension of the story and is not as memorable as the major tensions introduced in the 1st and 2nd Act even though her needing to let go of Jack in order to survive is the true climax of the film.

Mapping out your room

Maps are incredibly important when planning an IPE, but you won't be limited to just mapping out the physical space in a room. Because a great IPE changes as the players interact with it, so also should the map components. Your map should help you chart the progression of the game as well as the general game atmosphere.

When planning your map, it is important to remember that one of the greatest strengths of an IPE is you can really play with the concept of room layouts. One flipped wall, descending door, or even spinning room can magically change an entire layout. You can hide rooms inside of rooms and even have rooms move during the process of a game. That's why the puzzle progression of a room is the heart of mapping out the game, even more than the physical layout. In planning your puzzle progression, you can further develop the spacing of your anchor points, elements of expression, and doors. You should prepare to experiment with your map as much as possible, because once you are building the game you are increasingly locked into the choices you've made. While certain elements of expression and even puzzles can change, the general flow of your game cannot. For example, it would be incredibly difficult to add a fourth room to a game once construction had begun.

Puzzle Progression Map

The puzzle progression map is the most important map in identifying potential conflicts in the flow of your room. In every room there are puzzles that the players will need to stop and work on, puzzles that are quickly solved, and puzzles that advance the story or present more puzzle opportunities. You want to make sure that these moments do not overlap too much, because players typically don't want to miss out on special moments in the room by accident.

The layout of your room should have active puzzles marked in light green and the clues to the active puzzles marked in dark green. You want to be sure that the clues to your puzzles are in the same general vicinity and can be clearly grouped together by the players. Larger interface puzzles will typically be for assembly, observational, and sensory puzzles and so will have larger green areas. It is important to ensure that the area is covered in a way that ensures good player progression.

There should be at least a two to three ratio of clues to active puzzles to help guide players, but, as a general rule, if a clue could possibly exist in your environment, it should exist. Interesting environments have labels, notes, and directions inside of them. Your players need every possible context clue to solve your puzzles and so you should make sure you have given it to them.

A good puzzle progression for a room should come in three acts, with each act having the team feel stronger and cleverer when solving the next set of puzzles. You want to be careful about splitting the direction of the group on the left and right side of the map, especially in the first act when people are still likely to be in one group when solving puzzles. You also want to be careful when hiding puzzles behind walls or objects because the average group will have a difficult time noticing it. The more hidden the puzzles the more you will need clues to call attention to it.

As the game shifts to the second act, different portions of your puzzle map should light up. This most commonly is because a new room has opened up for players but it can also be because the nature of your one-room game has shifted. Different clues should become active in the room in a way clear and distinctive to players. Because the second act provides a new energy you should make sure that the puzzle progression is spaced different then the first time. Now would be a good time to introduce a more complicated puzzle progression for players.

The final act should have the most decisive moments and so should usually be centered around a smaller number of climactic, final puzzles. Groups will typically not want to search for relevant information at this point of the game so it helps if the puzzles and clues rely on patterns set during previous portions of the game. The most important issue is that the final puzzle really feels final to the players and so they all solve it together and do not miss the finale special effects.

Points and Walls Layout

Once an ideal puzzle progression has been imagined for a room, it's time to review how the elements of expression react with the puzzles. Now is the time to really brainstorm with the presentation of your puzzles and what will make them come more alive for the players. The best way to do this is to review the "points" and "walls" layout. There are different types of points and walls to keep track of, but they all are basically the points of view that your players will be seeing. The more you envision the space and the objects inside of it, the more you will really be able to view your room as a show for the players. To this end, each of the points will compose of basically long, medium, and close-up shots, just like in a movie. You can even take the mapping a step further and design a storyboard for your room if you like. The more you're really imagining an adventure and not just an environment, the better.

Presentation Points

Presentation points are the longshots of the room. They give the players clear access to the game's primary pathway and the clearest progression goals of the storyline. Not every room will have multiple presentation points, but every room will have at least one: when players enter the room. As soon as you enter a room you will scan for the most important elements. This moment of taking it all in should be most carefully planned by designers. These are the panoramic moments, the chance to take a sweeping view of the entire environment.

There are no interactive elements at presentation points, but several discussion points should be inside the highlighted range and easily approached by the players. Players usually like to have a bit of space between the presentation point and ideal decision points, giving them a chance to "descend the mountain" before making decisions about what to do. A presentation point example would be entering a restaurant and seeing the table section and bar section all at once. The party could then gather and decide whether they wanted to sit at the table or bar at that point. Or, if you entered a playground, you would like to see all the available stations to play with all at once before moving forward to make a decision.

Decision points

The medium shot of the room in which discussion can take place among the players about what puzzles to tackle. Left or right, enter or exit, be good or bad, interact or pass. Every room will have several decision points. These are the points when players can decide to engage in a puzzle or split off and try to do something else. A presentation point will always have the players moving forward to all the possible puzzles. A decision point will have them split apart and deliberately leave one behind. In the restaurant, this will be entering the table area and clearly not choosing to be in the bar area.

Always make the decision points as clear as possible so players will understand that they are making deliberate choices. If there are too many decision points at once in front of the players then it is a good time to pursue adding more wayfinding walls. Decision points make up all the secondary pathways and the clear engagement choices for the players to all of the anchor points, therefore they are always paired with the wayfinding walls that help guide the players along their way. While technically any position in the room could contain decision arrows, it is best to trace them from a clear presentation point because that is going to be the most likely path players take. You won't need to focus too much on obscure viewpoints in the room because every room will require some final adjustments in the actual construction. Fixing obscure points will also not require the elaborate decorations used in the construction of wayfinding walls so they are less of a concern.

Decision points are also the best places for story moments to happen as more people will be able to see them clearly. Decision points are right in front of bottleneck moments and doors in the game, so adding a video or audio update will be easily noticed by players. If a story moment happens at a presentation point then it necessarily needs to be more sweepingly expressive, such as watching day turn to night or watching a storm form or disburse. Therefore, most story moments that will be shared by the player will happen at decision points. Using our restaurant example, the host would approach the party once they entered the table section and invite them to choose between sitting at a booth or a table. The party could use the host's guidance to look at both the table and booth before making their final decision.

Wayfinding Walls

Wayfinding Walls are always paired with decision points because they help frame the places where the players will be discussing the puzzles. They are all elements that bring flavor and life to the game space but clearly do not contain puzzles themselves. They can sometimes contain clues or hidden clues but usually are just the decorations that make the room more engaging. Their elements of expression will typically be placemaking, subdivision, and negative space. They encourage the players to keep moving and make a decision. They are always inviting but rarely provoke the desire for intensive study, so they help guide players to the actual puzzles. Wayfinding walls can also accommodate storytelling as they are great elements to alter during the game or have an audio or visual event play. This would be a water feature in the restaurant on the way to the tables. The water feature makes the room feel more inviting and regal, but it would not cause the guests to extensively view it.

Using wayfinding walls doesn't just help fill a space but actually helps us search a room. If every object and structure seems to be connected to a puzzle then people will have a difficult time deciding how to proceed or what is important and unfocused exploration quickly becomes tedious. Wayfinding elements include sculptures, clocks, gyroscopes, abundant machinery, cages of animals, gates, portals, curtains, bridges, stairs, slides, archways, tunnels, and plants. In general, they are anything that make an area seem bursting with life. It is possible that wayfinding elements can eventually reveal puzzles hidden inside them, but until they become puzzles and switch to anchor points, they should clearly not have interfaces, locks, or compartments.

Anchor Points

Anchor points are where puzzles are presented in all their glory and players can focus completely on solving them, so these are the close-up shots. When you're solving a puzzle you are not able to focus on anything else. Anchor points can also be places where hints are shown to the players as most hints will completely absorb player's attentions as well. While it is possible to have story elements as anchor points, it is not recommended because it will be hard for most of the players to see it. If an anchor point does have a story element then the story element should be able to still clearly be seen through the player activating it.

To finish our restaurant example, it is the actual table where you order and consume your meal. Typically you don't move to the next table until you've finished your first meal, and so it is with puzzles. It is also, of course, why people are there so don't be surprised at the players with tunnel vision who don't spend enough time appreciating the wayfinding walls you've set up along the way. You'll always have players that will admire them to balance out the players that only have eyes for interfaces.

Two Player Anchor Point

One of the most important parts of IPE games is the ability to have unique puzzle interfaces. Some of the most unique puzzles available require two people to complete them, usually working from opposite sides of a wall or opposite ends of a wall. These puzzles require unique considerations in layouts, especially how the wayfinding walls might help guide players into playing the interface correctly. Typically, the more two player anchor points make communication easier, the better. I personally encourage having at least one two player anchor point inside your room because they are almost always as great of a crowd pleaser as a good magnet puzzle.

Points Layout Examples

There are some standard layouts for points and walls in a room that you can use to give the players the best impression of the game they are about to play. While every room is different, starting with a standard layout and then tweaking it to your more specific ideas can be a good designing shortcut.

All movement encouraged

For this layout, there will be no wayfinding walls in the room. All movement will be encouraged at the presentation point and there will be no particular decision points either. This typically is not a fun room for players because it will be hard to present a story in a room like this and they will have a hard time knowing where to begin when no puzzles are given preference over others. However, if your puzzles are sufficiently fun this this simple design can still be a big crowd pleaser. I have played one puzzle room like this that I fondly remember and one that... well. When that company went out of business I wasn't surprised.

Forward movement encouraged

Forward movement is encouraged when players have wayfinding walls presented immediately on either side of a presentation point and an anchor point directly in front of them. This makes the anchor point especially prominent. This can be a great beginning room with a very prominent puzzle, but it is not wise to have active puzzle elements obscured in a setup like this because the strong presentation of the puzzle will make players believe they can immediately solve it. I once had a game use this set-up for an Egypt room but also obscure information we needed to solve the puzzle under sand in the floor. It was much harder to begin searching for the additional information we needed because of the points and walls construction.

Left and right movement encouraged

With a wayfinding wall in the middle of the room, the decision points are going to be stronger at either side of it. This is a good room if there are distinctive sections or trials as players will have more reason to pause before making a decision. A statue is a good example of this layout. An intimidating statue in the middle of the room makes it more clear that players will be trying a trial to their left or their right.

Extreme left and right movement

Wayfinding walls can create extreme decision points. In this case, having a wayfinding wall that blocks most of the presentation point immediately requires players to make a left or right decision, and is more likely to cause the players to immediately split off into multiple groups. This is fun in claustrophobic rooms or spy game rooms.

Backwards movement encouraged

If wayfinding walls block the initial sides and the middle of the room then players will need to turn around to discover the puzzles, either through cracks in the wayfind walls or on the very back of the room. This can create a more immersive world experience but also makes it more difficult for players to orient themselves. It is a better setup for more fantasy world rooms or if players use a ramp to descend into the world.

No movement encouraged

If wayfinding elements block all the anchor points in a room then no movement will be encouraged. Players will have to explore to find the anchor points hidden behind each wall. Players will have a greater game atmosphere for the room but puzzle selection will be completely randomized and the game flow much harder to track. Players may also overly inspect wayfinding walls looking for puzzles in this case. But this would be a heck of a Stonehenge game set up.

Centered room movement

Centered room movement uses wayfinding walls to draw players into the room and towards certain puzzles but then surrounds them with puzzles, creating a more heightened decision-making experience after the initial presentation. This is better for a submarine or spaceship style game, where the controls in the center of the room surrounded by visuals of the environment make sense.

Guided two player anchor point movement

While there are some individual puzzles in the corners of this room, the two player anchor point is deliberately highlighted both by being prominent in the presentation point but also by having wayfinding walls that guide the players to both sides of the anchor point. This is a fun experience for tackling a rogue computer AI or winning a larger than life arcade puzzle.

Wall of two player anchor points

In this example, there is a wall of two player anchor points that will need to be engaged by players one by one. To make the puzzles more prominent to the players, they are sandwiched between wayfinding walls and create an entirely separate unit. This is an especially strong set-up for when players need to feel like they are taking down a complicated system, such as a complicated machine. By rewarding multiple points of communication the players have a chance to really engage the puzzles they face.

Points and walls layouts used to confirm ride Layout

A ride layout can be traced over a points and walls layout by first tracing the different directions people are likely to use when going from anchor point to anchor point and then drawing another master line on top of it. The more you can see whether you are introducing players to a "spaghetti" or "there and back" layout, the more you can tweak your puzzle placement and create a smoother experience for players.

Oppositional Elements map

Track the opposition design elements in your room by having arrows point to the "opposite" element. That way you can see the use of pin-balling, stratification, subdivision, continuation, and so on. You can also see if any elements have yet to be balanced by their opposition. There should be a lot of visual draws in your room, and so there should be many opposing points of view: masculine/feminine, busy/calm, fast/slow, loud/quiet, wide/narrow, wet/dry, old/new, organic/geometric, scary/reassuring, clean/dirty, hot/cold, harmonious/discordant

When I opposition mapped my room, I found two environmental errors that I had overlooked even though I had thought through the room design dozens of times and had watched dozens of groups play the room at that point. But I had some spare hours that day so I walked through the entire experience and drew all the arrows until I discovered my missed opportunities.

The first was a missing clue. I knew people were having trouble recognizing that a podium was a puzzle interface, but it wasn't until I marked the podium as "masculine" as opposed to a feminine mirror on the opposite side of the corridor that I realized it would make sense to boost the masculine further and label the podium. Labelling the podium would also make sense in-character because the podium's creator would want low-level employees to be aware of its existence. Remember: any time a clue could reasonably exist in an environment, it should be in the environment.

The second error I found was a missing wayfinding wall. There was geometric section of the game that could be counterbalanced with a more organic design. By slightly shifting the active puzzle space to make way for the wayfinding wall, I could put in a wall of mannequins dressed in costumes. This would make sense in the world because that part of the game was more the "storage" area of the theater, but it would also bring a contrast of "free flowing" to the more rigid bolted element on the opposite side. Without searching for the contrasts in the room I would never have been able to come to that conclusion.

GETTING YOUR FINAL GRADE

It's time to pull everything together and see what your final grade is. More importantly, it's time to see if you can improve your score. Attractions can be graded according to how they conform to the entertainment analytics described in the previous chapters of this book. While art will always have individual subjectivity in its expression (meaning it IS okay if someone doesn't like your room just because it doesn't "feel right"), there are a lot of ways to confirm that your game has surpassed the standard of performance. We might not always like a particular restaurant, but if they are up to code, have a good décor, and a well-thought out menu we're going to get very close.

Bell Curve for Room Success

Every team plays a room a bit differently, but ultimately a bell curve can be created by tracking the ideal time and number of hints for a room and combining them into an ideal score. Most rooms are best with a bell curve score that has a peak around fifty minutes and with two hints used. These hints should be stronger than simple nudges by the game master or game host but instead true breaks in the game's flow, either by directly telling players what to do or solving a task for them. If most people solve the room in faster than 40 minutes then it is too easy and if most people cannot solve the room at all it is too hard. If people are never needing hints the room is too easy but if they are constantly needing hints then it is too hard. That is why a bell curve of charting time against hints is the most useful at confirming a room is successfully operating. A few groups will win with incredibly fast times and a few will lose no matter how much you help them, but the clear majority of players must be inside the curve to confirm that the room is successfully calibrated.

Out-of-world elements

Out-of-world elements are anything that would not be naturally part of the game environment but are there specifically to guide the player's performance or inorganically explain the story. This includes television screens in environments that would find their placement off-putting. This is not just for fantasy setting rooms, but rooms in which the use of television monitors wouldn't connect with the game's story. A museum may have a television display, but it wouldn't have a television display of the player's countdown time. Giving the players their own personal handheld tablet to track their time can keep the environment organic while keeping the players informed of their chief obstacles.

Voiceovers are often used to point to out-of-world elements, usually as game masters want to draw attention to certain anchor points. However, this damages the story of the game and should only be used when players need to specifically be warned against damaging equipment they are already close to breaking, not to help generally guide them. Having the game master contact the players in ways that fit in the world's parameters, such as through written messaged or with a call on the phone, better uses the world's reality and engages the players.

Posted rules and sticker warnings are some of the worst out-of-world element offenders. While there are ways these elements can be handled inside the world, they are often parts of larger issues either with the props or the puzzles themselves. The flow of the game should be simplified or the props reinforced in durability instead of posting stickers. Mark every out-of-world element in your game. If you can't replace it immediately see if there are ways to replace it down the road.

Irregular Puzzle layout

Irregular puzzle layouts do not use any noticeable pattern for ride layouts to help guide the game's flow. While it is impossible to completely predict the motion of a room, an ideal flow should be able to be charted by using the points and walls layout and creating a puzzle progression map. Is the layout too stretched or squeezed to fit in the space? Do players go back and forth too many times in the room sections ruining a chance of harmony in the game? Are there too many decision points or wayfinding walls? The key is experimentation during the planning stage and seeing if there are better ways to have puzzles fit your space. Can the size of puzzles be changed? Can their order be changed? Would another ride layout or intensity structure be more fun? There may very well be real limits in the chosen environment for your game so be sure that the elements you are able to alter and chose fit the environment as perfectly as possible.

Poor Puzzle Ratio

Poor puzzle ratios are games that have too many anchor points that are the same type of puzzle, or do not have a good grouping of "Freebie" to "E ticket" attractions in the rooms. If a room does not have any larger attractions, experienced players will be disappointed in the room, even if the "A ticket" and "B ticket" puzzles are of incredibly high value. Similar, larger attractions need to be balanced with smaller attractions for the sake of build-up, rest, and pacing. The more players sense a room changing in the challenges it gives to players, the more it can be an exciting experience even if the room has a lower budget. If players are told their puzzles are important for saving the world then they be willing to assign them a high value for the sake of the story alone.

Good Player misdirection

Red herrings need to be carefully placed and controlled. Players will already be likely to associate wayfinding walls and random props as clues for puzzles, so especially arcane and complicated wayfinding elements may only distract and frustrate them. Every guest will often bring unique ideas of misdirection based on their own game and story bias as well as previous game experiences. Sometimes, previous rooms will have even trained your players against your room. If a previous room gave players a lot of instructions to never unplug the equipment, than an in-game prop that needs to be unplugged to "override the system" will be the very last thing your players attempt to do. Hiding props under furniture or expecting players to "tear" at a section of the room will also go against the training of experienced players.

Ways that misdirection can be created include places where tools seem to need to be used, extraneous story points, or possible places to use strange technology. For example, having a golf club that is used to unhook an object that is hooked to the ceiling and never to hit any actual golf balls will still have the players looking to putt with it in the room even after they have "used" it as a tool. They will still expect and search for the normal use.

The greatest offender is storytelling, which is another reason why story elements should always be minimized in a room and shown visibly as much as possible. Giving players mysterious story point information like, "In 1875, Victoria fell in love with the color red" will have players entering the year date, Victoria's name, and searching for the color red the entire game. Players will try to consider all information game worthy.

Misdirection can also come from poorly cued lock interfaces. Using a Master Lock directional combination lock to input a very long sequence will have players doubting the puzzle's answer unless they know that the directional lock can have up to 18 individual inputs and how to reset the lock. They will not suspect that the lock interface naturally failed from being hard to use.

Retrace moments

While retracing moments can be a lot of fun for players, unnecessary retracing due to confusing directions or too subtle game design should be minimized. During live play testing, retracing should be noted because it will reveal players either not having enough interest in a puzzle to complete it in one session or not understanding the room's requirements enough to want to engage in puzzles. Be prepared with good plan "B"s if you lose your player's interest faster than anticipated. I know that I have personally been disappointed in a few of my puzzles when presented to the general public but was unfortunately too far along in the game's construction to offer up a viable secondary solution. The players now suffer through a slower moment in the game then they should.

Staff access and control

It is important to plan and build a smooth room reset for staff so that the next team can start playing as soon as possible. It is also important to have easy maintenance to keep the room in top working condition, but neither of these focuses should ever cut into the game experience itself. The reset locks and maintenance controls for staff should be invisible to players. The convenience of the staff should never make for awkward gameplay. There are many clever ways to hide staff controls in the environment, including using FOBS, fake panels, and screws. Just try and return to the reset issues later in the game's operation. I was able to return to game elements and come up with very valuable tricks for reset that depended on magician principles months after initially opening my game. The secret is to hide reset values in plain sight, like with fake paneling or out-of-reach tools.

AND NOW? THE FINAL SECRET

True to any mystery book, I've saved the best secrets for last, but they've been built on all the revelations that have come before. So why not try and keep all this information to myself and try to use it in my rooms alone? Because I know this moment is bigger than myself and the work I can do. I want everyone who is willing to use the best possible tools and give their customers the most fun. Because I bet you can discover a new secret and push the industry further.

I know this books valuable to designers because I constantly use it myself. There's a lot of tools to use in creating a puzzle after all! And I know I'm not done yet. I review the different ideas here and see how to better refine them and explain them year after year. And they help remind me what I'm missing on a puzzle I've just created or a concept I'm exploring. I wrote this book to challenge myself and it has worked. My designs have become amazingly better since working on this book. Again and again, as I've thought over principles I've outlined here, I've come up with ways to improve my room and make it more exciting, more logical, and much, much more fun.

Writing this book was my own best chance to keep learning and keep improving, because I love how exciting it is to sort the objective from the subjective experiences in professional puzzle development. I've learned what's fun for a lot of people versus what is fun for a few. A lot of puzzles I've grown up with and assumed everyone loved (or at least new about) have been met with blanker faces than you see on our haunted mannequins. But when I find a puzzle people really enjoy it's always fun to watch it click in their minds as they solve it. I still sometimes hold my breath waiting for a player to discover that "eureka" moment. The real truth is that every one of my customers is a personal hero of mine because they've sought at puzzles as something fun to do. Think about it! They give their money and time to share in something I love. I had to write a book that honors them and I want to shape the industry the best I can to honor them too.

Interactive Puzzle Exhibits are the new artwork platform of our times, incorporating all forms of entertainment that came before them from our games, movies, and lives. All the fun moments we imagined ourselves doing on the playground are now ours to experience in a format assembled from all the entertainment interfaces that came before it: board games, paper puzzles, team sports, video games, and theme park rides. Like any great form of art, it reminds us of the old while creating something entirely new. And in creating the next step in entertainment it will inspire us to even greater entertainment heights and even more exciting futures for entertainment experiences.

The final secret is that this is the beginning of the next truly new thing. And I'm excited to help the world find it! Will there be little league IPE teams? Will we finally write virtual reality games that capture a wide market? Will we create holodecks that turn on their masters? Or will the work we do in this industry just reinvigorate existing artforms? I've no idea! I just know when you can turn an individual dream into a dream shared by a team it's no longer a dream but a work of art. One day there will be a new paintbrush and canvas; a new lock and key. The clock is already set, so let's get solving!

Printed in Great Britain
by Amazon